Asian
Green

For Master Cheng Yen and Tze Sifu,
TZU CHI Buddhist Foundation, Hualien

Ching-He Huang

Photography by Tamin Jones

Kyle Books

Asian

Everyday plant-based
recipes inspired
by the East

Green

An Hachette UK Company
www.hachette.co.uk

First published in the Great Britain in 2021
by Kyle Books, an imprint of
Octopus Publishing Group Limited
Carmelite House
50 Victoria Embankment
London EC4Y 0DZ
www.kylebooks.co.uk
www.octopusbooksusa.com

Distributed in the US by
Hachette Book Group
1290 Avenue of the Americas
4th and 5th Floors
New York, NY 10104

Distributed in Canada by
Canadian Manda Group
664 Annette St.
Toronto, Ontario, Canada M6S 2C8

Editorial Director: Judith Hannam
Publisher: Joanna Copestick
Copy Editor: Tara O'Sullivan
Editor: Jenny Dye
Art Direction: Evi O. Studio | Evi O.
Design: Evi O. Studio | Susan Le and Kait Polkinghorne
Photography: Tamin Jones
Food styling: Aya Nishimura and Rosie Reynolds
Props styling: Wei Tang
Production: Lucy Carter and Nic Jones

ISBN 978-0-85783-634-2

A CIP catalogue record for this book is available from the British Library.

Printed and bound in China

10 9 8 7 6 5 4 3 2 1

Introduction

Hello! Thanks so much for choosing *Asian Green*. I hope it will inspire you on your plant-based journey and give you some fun when it comes to those important meal times!

The recipes are designed with busy people like you in mind, to help you either go more veggie or completely plant based. They are simple enough for everyday, yet sufficiently gourmet for entertaining too, with all the ingredients widely available from major supermarkets. Perhaps most importantly of all, they have also been designed for optimal health, mindfulness and balance. These recipes are not going to cost you the earth, or Mother Nature. A win-win!

The dishes use mainly fresh produce but also ingredients such as tofu, seitan, pulses, beans and grains to give you nutritionally balanced meals. I have categorised them into Satisfying Breakfasts & Morning Drinks, Nourishing Soups, Fresh & Exotic Salads, Fast & Furious, Warm & Comforting, Sharing Plates and Sweet Tooth.

My husband, Jamie, is vegan. From birth, he suffered from asthma and eczema, but, in 2017, after adopting a plant-based diet which he continues to follow, his symptoms disappeared within three months and to this day haven't returned! Having experienced first-hand the transformation of my husband's health, I am more than ever convinced by the age-old Chinese maxim that 'food is medicine'. The healing power of plants and their ability to reduce inflammation, restore, nourish and replenish are the inspirations behind this book.

Good health starts with healing one's body (and mind) with 'pure' food that is kind to the planet and us. Whether you are already plant based or just starting out on your journey, I have you covered for flavourful eating, with lots of tips and tricks to help you along the way.

The dishes are varied and wide-ranging, as I've taken inspiration from all across Asia. Whatever your reason for going plant based, I wish you success and I hope this book helps to increase your cooking repertoire.

A green lotus flower is deemed as a beautiful gift for anyone trying to improve their life and start good habits. I hope you see this as my small sharing gift to you. Let's get started.

Love, Ching xxx

Why Go Plant-based?

For a few years now, I have been toying with the idea of becoming fully vegan. Initially, I was very tentative, but gradually the benefits of a plant-based diet seeped into my consciousness. Two things in particular had an overwhelming impact.

First, it was the documentary *Forks Over Knives*, which showed how two doctors, Dr T. Colin Campbell and Dr Caldwell Esselstyn, cured their patients' chronic heart disease and reversed their diabetes within three months by encouraging them to cut out saturated animal products and follow a plant-based diet.

Then my husband, Jamie, became vegan. He had been going through a tough time and had begun focussing on more spiritual things. Reading books such as *Conversations with God* by Neale Donald Walsch and *Adventures Beyond the Body* by William Bulhman gave him a deep compassion for animals. Before you close this book and say, 'Ching's become a real hippie', the changes I saw in Jamie were too incredible to ignore!

Jamie had suffered from asthma and eczema since birth. From the time I began dating him, he never left the house without worrying about whether he was carrying an inhaler, not to mention the need to take his preventative too. However, within three months of switching to a plant-based diet, his asthma disappeared – together with his eczema! Going vegan profoundly changed both his health and the quality of his life.

It got me thinking so much about what we don't know about the power of plants.

Plants are usually seen as 'weak', but their power is clearly transformative, as is demonstrated by Jamie, who is now 'stronger' than ever. The improvement in his health has been a huge source of inspiration to me and that's why I wanted to write this book. On a deep level, Jamie's search and journey to optimal health were a result of the committed and often challenging choices he made every mealtime, every day, 365 days a year. When he started, he experienced peer pressure, not only from me, but from his family and friends. We quizzed him at almost every meal we shared together. I know it was very difficult for him, but he had the courage to follow his natural instincts.

For Buddhists, the lotus flower symbolises rebirth and enlightenment. Out of muddy waters, this incredible plant re-blooms each morning without residue on its petals. Its seed can lie dormant for 2,000 years, and then germinate and grow – a truly powerful plant! In many ways, it symbolises the potential in us all to awaken, no matter how long it takes, and the patience that is required to reach one's destiny. Jamie's daily journey in search of health reminds me of the challenges of the lotus seed. He was surrounded by delicious temptations (my meaty cooking!) yet undeniably his health wasn't just improving: it was blossoming, like the lotus flower. All of which made me consider the transformative possibilities for our health, society and our planet: if we were all like the lotus flower, how beautiful could the world become?

To see it happen to Jamie was one thing, but I also had to experience it for myself. It isn't difficult for me to eat a more plant-based diet. I love vegetables and I'm a chef by profession, so I know how to prepare and cook them. I have also always been conscious of the need to eat well and have felt a responsibility to create recipes that are healthy and balanced, using seasonal ingredients that are as kind to the planet as possible. I'd soon got tired of cooking two different meals, one for Jamie and one for me, so I'd settled into being flexitarian, cooking and eating vegan at home, except when testing recipes or researching new ones. For the past few years, I have eaten a plant-based diet about 80 per cent of the time, and for the rest always used good-quality meat or fish.

At the time of writing the synopsis of this book, I was happy with the idea that I would always be a flexitarian, having the best of both worlds and being able to eat meat whenever I had a craving for it. However, when I came to write the book, and particularly after Covid-19 and lockdown hit the UK, I began to think seriously about who I am, my fragility, the world around me, and what my work means to me. Also, more importantly, what I stand for, my contribution to the planet, and how to live a more meaningful existence! In a video I watched on YouTube, the

Indian yogi Sadhguru talked about love, and how, during lockdown, if we could improve ourselves and make ourselves 10 per cent better than when we started, this would be a good time to take action. All my work dried up because of Covid-19 – my teaching classes, demo events and public appearances were all cancelled. My recipe development work also came to a natural end as projects reached completion. Everything just stopped, except delivering this plant-based cookbook. It was as if the universe was challenging me to stop procrastinating and find out whether I could become fully vegan. I had begun to feel I was being slightly hypocritical doing a completely plant-based book when I wasn't all-in myself, and, I reasoned with myself, I was almost there wasn't I?

Before Covid-19, there was always the next project, the next meeting, as well as the

next client lunch to distract me from becoming vegan. It was a no brainer really. There was no better time to do it. Even though I knew I was a 'bad' Buddhist, morally it had never sat well with me that a sentient being had to give their life for me to survive, especially when, as a human, I have free will and choice. So I made the leap and can honestly report that I feel so much better. As my Buddhist master says, all life on earth is energy, we are energy. Emotions are energies-in-motion. So, if all are sentient on earth, and all feel emotion, if we consume life that has suffered, then we consume the energy of suffering and that is absorbed into us. If we consume without suffering, that negative emotion cannot consume us.

Even if you are not on a vegan journey, eating more consciously can have a dramatic impact on your carbon footprint. Of course, eating consciously means nations need to be more self-sufficient, growing more locally produced food to reduce air miles, but if everyone switched overnight to a diet that consisted of 90 per cent vegetables and 10 per cent very good-quality meat or fish, it would be a more sustainable path for our planet.

Doctors recommend eating ten portions of fruit and veg a day. I remember travelling to Okinawa in 2015 (to film my TV show *Ching's Amazing Asia*). This small and humble island is home to some of the oldest and healthiest centenarians in the world, who live predominantly on legumes and vegetables, with the addition

of some fish. The 'science' is there – true stories of experiments and health transformations from people all over the world.

It would be untruthful to say I haven't had the occasional craving for Peking duck and cheap chocolate, but I have found that there are delicious plant-based substitutes for almost every one of my favourite junk food cravings. I've therefore included vegan versions of every one of my favourite meat dishes, including Japanese Tofu, Mushroom & Pickle Hand Rolls (page 50), Wok-fried Orange-Soy Sticky Sprouts & Wild Rice Salad (page 56), Sticky Hoisin Broccoli with Toasted Almonds (page 96), Miso-roasted Cauliflower with Chickpea, Carrot & Noodle Salad (page 60), Waikiki Bowl (page 67), Five-spice Mixed Mushroom Soba Chow Mein (page 80), General Tso's Cauliflower & Sweetcorn (page 94), Spicy Tempeh & Kimchi Stir-fry (page 108), Chunky Smoked Tofu & Broccoli Korean-style Ram-don (page 126), Vietnamese Mushroom & Asparagus Raw Spring Rolls (page 154) and Peking Mushroom Pancakes (page 162).

And look, it's okay to have an occasional wobble. Just get back on it again the next day. Like the lotus flower, tomorrow is another day, another opportunity to reset, revive and grow to being a better version of your old self. In times of wobble, these encouraging words by my favourite Chinese philosopher, Lao Tze, bring me back in alignment:

Watch your thoughts; they become words;
Watch your words; they become actions;
Watch your actions; they become habits;
Watch your habits; they become character;
Watch your character; it becomes your destiny.

How What We Eat Affects the Planet

I wanted to write this book because I can see a win-win both for the health of the planet and for humans. Going wholly plant-based is a daily committed choice, but a sustainable one if the intention is there. We can choose not to inflict pain on ourselves and others by choosing kindness in all our habits. The habit closest to home is what we choose to eat.

We are living through a period known as the sixth mass extinction, caused by human activity. We have killed half of all wildlife in the last 40 years and 83 per cent of wild mammals, due to overpopulation and the fact that 26 per cent of the earth's surface is used for grazing livestock.

Perhaps the greatest danger is climate warming. A catastrophic 2 per cent rise in global temperatures will displace much of the global population. The trapping of greenhouse gases such as carbon dioxide and methane in the earth's atmosphere continues to melt the ice caps, causing flooding and climate disasters. With carbon levels in the atmosphere at their highest in 650,000 years, reducing our footprint is an urgent matter.

Is cutting out meat good for health?

Atherosclerosis, otherwise known as plaque in your arteries, is associated with a high intake of meat, fat and carbohydrates, and is a leading cause of death in the United States. Eating a diet high in red meat also raises the risk of death from cancer or heart disease. Eating processed meat further increases the risk of cancer, and WHO (World Health Organization) lists it as carcinogenic.

And what about fish?

Tragically, 90 per cent of large ocean predatory fish have been killed and 87 per cent of fish populations are over-exploited. For every 450g (16oz) of fish caught, 1.8kg (4lb) of marine species are discarded as by-kill. At our present rate of consumption, the world will run out of saltwater fish by 2048. So, while fish is a good source of omega-3, it is better to go direct to the source and eat seaweed or algae supplements, to give our oceans a chance to restore and heal.

Should we eat more soy? Isn't soy the cause of deforestation in the Amazon?

The humble soybean has sustained millions for centuries in the Far East, and continues to do so today. Wonderfully nutritious, it can be used to make soy sauce, miso, edamame, tofu, soy milk, fermented soy pastes and soybean noodles. It is high in protein and a good source of phytoestrogen. I have consumed large amounts of soy in my diet since I was a child. If you are allergic to soy, there are plenty of grains from other legumes – lentils, beans, chickpeas, yellow peas – that are also nutrient dense and rich in fibre.

90 per cent of the Amazon rainforest's total deforestation is for animal agriculture and 80 per cent of soy grown in the Amazon is fed to animals – only 6 per cent of soya produced globally is for humans. By reducing the number of animals we consume, we could feed another 3.5 billion people.

Eating Mindfully

Eating mindfully is perhaps the single most difficult thing to do when we are running at 100 miles per hour in our daily lives. It requires dedication, knowledge, awareness and self-discipline. To master what we eat is to master our health. Here are a few simple words of wisdom that have helped me and Jamie. Knowing these will help you to eat more wisely.

Simplicity, freshness and seasonality

My grandparents live frugally on a farm, cooking simple, vibrant dishes in tune with the seasons that feature minimal meat and fish, but an abundance of fresh fruit and vegetables. This book is a celebration of this Asian way of eating.

I strongly recommend sourcing local organic fresh produce. Most Asian storecupboard staples, however, arrive by boat, which is more sustainable.

The rainbow way

Eating a variety of fruit and vegetables every day is key and ideally you should eat all the colours of the rainbow. Aim for a diet of 50 per cent of fresh fruit and veg and at least five portions of fruit and five portions of vegetables per day. The remainder of your diet should be 25 per cent protein and 25 per cent grains. Aim for a diverse range of ingredients from spices to grains, plant proteins and seasonal vegetables.

Know your protein

Protein is needed for enzymes, hormones, antibodies and to build and repair our muscles. There is a myth that the plant-based diet is low in protein but this is simply not true. Animals such as cows, sheep and chickens get their protein from grains and nuts. Vegans cut out the 'middle men' and go direct to source.

There is protein in almost all foods. Seitan, which is made from wheat, is a rich source with 22.5g (¾oz) of protein per serving. Many brands offer plant-based protein, but it is best to keep it fresh, and to eat mostly legumes, fresh fruit and veg, plus a selection of these Asian plant-based proteins.

Dofu/Tofu

The Mandarin transliteration is Doufu, the Japanese is tofu. It contains all nine essential amino acids and is an excellent source of iron, calcium, manganese, selenium and phosphorus, and of copper, magnesium, vitamin B1 and zinc.

Whether you choose fresh, fried, firm or smoked tofu, try to get organic tofu or that made from sprouted soy, and stay away from GM versions. Tofu is processed, so vary your intake to get a healthy balance. On average 3–4 times a week is fine. Use my tofu recipe on page 195 if you fancy having a go.

Firm and smoked tofu are delicious in stews, stir-fries, braised dishes, curries and salads. Silken tofu is perfect for making desserts and creamy dressings. The beauty of tofu is that it's what you add to the dish that determines its flavour.

Seitan has a great texture and can be added to stir-fries, soups, salads, or even roasted or baked. You can make your own (see page 194) or buy it ready-cooked and preserved in ginger soy brine from supermarkets.

Like tofu, tempeh is made predominantly of soy beans. It is fermented, and less processed than tofu, but much chewier. Tempeh can be roasted, pan-fried, baked or stir fried. You can find it in most supermarkets. Some textures include whole beans and/or chickpeas.

Vitamins and minerals

Vitamins are important when you go vegan. At times, we all run on empty and when stressed it's not always possible to eat well. I would therefore suggest that you take a daily vitamin supplement, in particular vitamins B6 and, as most people are deficient, a vitamin B12 booster. Also look out for foods like cereals and plant-based yoghurts that are fortified with vitamin B12.

Iron is a crucial mineral for healthy blood, and foods such as porridge oats, beans, lentils, dark chocolate, tofu, tempeh, watercress, almonds, Brazil nuts and seeds all contain good amounts.

Calcium is really important for strong bones and is found in beans, watercress, okra, broccoli, butternut squash and sweet potato.

Not spending enough time in the sun can lead to a deficiency in vitamin D, so you should get 15 minutes of sun in spring and summer, and increase your intake of foods fortified with vitamin D in the winter. Regular weight-bearing and resistance training exercises help strengthen the bones too.

Dark leafy greens – Brussels sprouts, kale, spinach – are rich sources of folate and iron. Greens are delicious simply steamed, but an easy way to get them into the diet is to put them in shakes or have them raw in salads. They are also a good source of omega-3, which helps the immune system and is good for heart health. A wholly plant-based diet can sometimes be deficient in omega-3, so ideally you should take omega-3 supplements 2–3 times a week.

80/20 rule

Choosing to eat well is a habit and if you choose to eat well 80 per cent of the time, you can enjoy treats 20 per cent of the time. It's all about balance and eating mindfully. Every recipe in this book includes macro nutrient analysis, so you can see exactly how much protein, fat, carbs and sugars you are consuming. There is nothing wrong with counting calories, but as you go on your healthy eating journey, you will intuitively grasp what your body needs.

Soy and plant-based milks

There are plenty of plant-based milks available for cereals, baking and drinking. Soy milk is made from soaked soy beans blended with water – I give a recipe on page 195. There are also different varieties of nut milks. I tend to drink coconut milk and soy milk and use oat or almond milk for baking.

Nutritional yeast

These dried yeast flakes have a deep savoury umami flavour. Some are fortified with vitamin B12. I keep a jar mixed with ground almonds, salt, pepper and shichimi togarashi pepper flakes for sprinkling on top of salads, soups and noodle dishes.

1.

Satisfying Breakfasts & Morning Drinks

Miso Corn & Sweet Potato Pancakes

Serves 2
(makes 10 pancakes)

10 min   10 min

Chinese pancakes, otherwise known as *bing*, are one of my favourite breakfasts. I miss the aunties selling these in the markets in Beijing, usually spring onion pancakes with an eggy crêpe. This is my version of this delicious brunch dish, made using shop-bought wholegrain pancakes, which you just need to steam for a few minutes in a small bamboo basket. The filling is so quick to wok up and is sweet, salty and more-ish. In the summer months, you can brush the corn with red miso and olive oil and roast it on the barbecue, but in the winter, cooking in the wok will still give you that smoky, charred flavour.

1 tbsp rapeseed oil

2.5cm (1in) piece of fresh root ginger, grated

1 large sweet potato, peeled and diced into 0.5cm (¼in) cubes

50ml (2fl oz) vegetable stock

1 tbsp unsalted sunflower spread

1 tsp red miso paste

340g (12oz) can sweetcorn, drained

1 tbsp tamari or low-sodium light soy sauce

1 tbsp golden syrup

1 tbsp mirin

pinch of chilli flakes

To serve

10 small shop-bought wheat-flour pancakes (or use little gem lettuce leaves)

2 spring onions, trimmed and sliced into julienne strips

sriracha, for drizzling (optional)

Place the pancakes in a small bamboo steamer and set over a pan half-filled with water. Close the lid and steam over a high heat for 5 minutes.

Meanwhile, heat a wok over high heat until smoking, and add the rapeseed oil. Once hot, add the ginger and stir for a few seconds, then add the sweet potato cubes and stir-fry for 2–3 minutes. Continue to cook, adding drops of vegetable stock as you go in order to steam-fry the sweet potato. Cook in this manner for another 2 minutes until the sweet potato is soft but still has bite. Push the sweet potato cubes to one side of the wok.

Add the sunflower spread and miso paste to the centre of the wok, then add the sweetcorn and mix to coat the sweetcorn kernels in the miso paste. Stir well until the miso has all dissolved. Season with tamari or light soy sauce and golden syrup, then add the mirin to loosen. Cook until slightly reduced, then toss the sweet potato and sweetcorn together for 30 seconds. Sprinkle with chilli flakes.

To serve, fold each pancake in half to form a semicircle, then in half again to make a shape like an ice-cream cone. Holding the cone between your thumb and forefinger, fill it with the sweet potato and sweetcorn mixture. Top with spring onion, drizzle over some sriracha (if you like) and eat immediately.

Wok-fried Long-stem Broccoli, Oyster Mushrooms, Tomatoes & Basil with Avocado

kcal — 313
carbs — 9.2g
protein — 8.2g
fat — 27.4g

Serves 2

10 min   2–3 min

This tasty breakfast is low in calories and packed full of nutrients: the mushrooms are high in antioxidants, the avocado and cashews are full of healthy fats, there is plenty of vitamin C in the juicy tomatoes, and the long-stem broccoli contains folic acid. Serve with sourdough toast and chilli-spiced baked beans on the side if you wish.

1 tbsp rapeseed oil

2 garlic cloves, finely chopped

100g (3½oz) long-stem broccoli, sliced on the angle into 2.5cm (1in) pieces

100g (3½oz) grey oyster mushrooms

6 cherry tomatoes, halved

1 tbsp tamari or low-sodium light soy sauce

pinch of freshly ground black pepper

small handful of basil, sliced

handful of toasted cashew nuts

1 avocado, peeled, stoned and sliced, to serve

Heat a wok over a high heat until smoking, then add the rapeseed oil. Once hot, add the garlic and stir-fry for a few seconds, then add the long-stem broccoli and oyster mushrooms and toss for 2–3 minutes until the vegetables have softened a little.

Add the cherry tomatoes and tamari or light soy sauce and stir-fry together briefly, then add the black pepper, basil and toasted cashew nuts and stir through.

Take off the heat and divide between two plates. Serve with the sliced avocado.

Ching's Tip — Try switching the broccoli for asparagus or baby spinach, depending on what is in season. If using baby spinach, add it at the end, as it wilts down in no time.

Courgetti Noodles in a Seaweed Mushroom Broth

Serves 2

10 min   10 min

Inspired by Japanese cold soba-style noodles, this is my own healthy seaweed broth, using courgetti as noodles. It is delicious and cleansing, and makes an ideal light brunch. It can be served hot or cold; to serve cold, simply let the broth cool before putting the dish together.

2 courgettes, trimmed and spiralised

1 tbsp toasted sesame seeds

1 spring onion, trimmed and finely sliced

4 dried nori sheets, torn

For the broth

2 dried shiitake mushrooms, washed

1 tsp vegetable bouillon powder

1 tbsp tamari or low-sodium light soy sauce

1 tbsp mirin

2 tbsp dried wakame seaweed

pinch of sea salt

1 tbsp toasted sesame oil

To serve

100g (3½oz) smoked tofu, drained, rinsed in cold water and diced

Begin by making the broth. Place a wok over a medium heat and add 750ml (25fl oz) boiling water, along with the shiitake mushrooms, bouillon powder, tamari or light soy sauce, mirin, wakame seaweed and sea salt. Bring to the boil, then reduce the heat to low. Simmer for 10 minutes, then stir in the toasted sesame oil.

Remove the wok from the heat and strain the mixture through a sieve, collecting the broth. Set aside the strained mushrooms and wakame seaweed.

Divide the spiralised courgette between two bowls. Pour over the broth (either hot or cold), then sprinkle over the sesame seeds and spring onion. Add the nori, which will dissolve into the broth.

Place the reserved mushrooms and wakame seaweed into separate small bowls, along with the smoked tofu, and serve alongside the broth as toppings.

Shiitake Tofu Scramble with Chives

kcal — 326
carbs — 6.3g
protein — 13.8g
fat — 27.0g

Serves 2

10 min   4 min

I love a tofu scramble. This one is so quick and easy, but full of flavour. It makes a perfect hot breakfast all year round. I like to serve it with sliced avocado on the side for extra nutrition.

1 tbsp rapeseed oil

2.5cm (1in) piece of fresh root ginger, grated

200g (7oz) firm tofu, drained and chopped into 1cm (½in) cubes

1 tbsp dark soy sauce

100g (3½oz) fresh shiitake mushrooms (choose ones that are small, thin and tender, with small caps), left whole

1 tbsp tamari or low-sodium light soy sauce

1 tsp toasted sesame oil

juice of 1 lemon

pinch of freshly ground black pepper

small bunch of chives, finely chopped

large handful of baby spinach leaves

To serve

large pinch of shichimi togarashi pepper flakes

1 avocado, peeled, stoned and sliced

Heat a wok over a high heat until smoking. Add the rapeseed oil and swirl it around in the wok. Once hot, add the ginger and stir for a few seconds, then add the tofu pieces and cook for 1 minute.

Season with dark soy sauce, then start to break up the tofu pieces using your spoon. Add the shiitake mushrooms and toss together for 20 seconds.

Stir in the tamari, sesame oil, lemon juice and black pepper, and sprinkle over the chopped chives.

Divide the baby spinach leaves between two plates and spoon the tofu scramble over the top. Sprinkle over some shichimi togarashi pepper flakes and serve immediately with the sliced avocado.

Xian-style Carrot, Potato & Spring Onion Hash

kcal — 797
carbs — 116.4g
protein — 18.0g
fat — 32.2g

Serves 2, or 4 to share

20 min 7 min

These carrot, potato and spring onion patties are inspired by the spicy flavours of Xian. The cumin, fennel, dried chillies and salt make them delicious and more-ish. Dipping the pitta breads into a spiced, salty seasoning before toasting them adds another level of flavour.

sunflower oil, for frying

4 pitta bread pockets

For the carrot, potato & spring onion hash

2 tbsp chia seeds

2 carrots, finely grated

2 large Maris Piper potatoes, peeled and finely grated

2 spring onions, trimmed and finely chopped

¼ tsp sea salt

1 tsp each cumin seeds and fennel seeds

pinch of dried chilli flakes

½ tsp ground turmeric

1 tbsp cornflour

For the sesame seasoning oil

1 tbsp toasted sesame oil

1 tsp each toasted black and toasted white sesame seeds

½ tsp vegetable bouillon powder

large pinch each of sea salt, cumin seeds, fennel seeds and dried chilli flakes

1 tbsp cornflour

To serve

2 tbsp sriracha

4 tbsp shop-bought vegan mayonnaise

4 iceberg lettuce leaves, finely shredded

Begin by making a chia 'egg'. Mix the chia seeds with 4 tbsp water in a small bowl. Let stand for 5 minutes before using.

Now transfer the chia 'egg' to a large bowl and add all the other hash ingredients. Stir well to combine. Wet your hands with a little water, then use them to shape the mixture into four evenly sized, round, flat patties. Set aside.

Heat a wok over a medium heat and pour in sunflower oil to a depth of about 0.5cm (¼in). Heat the oil to 150°C (300°F), then shallow-fry the patties for 1½ minutes on each side. Remove from the wok and set aside on a plate lined with kitchen paper to drain. Pour the used oil into a heatproof container. Leave to cool before discarding the oil. Wipe the wok with a piece of kitchen paper.

In a jug, combine the ingredients for the seasoning oil with 2 tbsp hot water.

Return the wok to a medium heat.

Take your first pitta bread pocket. Dip a brush in the seasoning oil and brush one side of the pitta. Place the pitta in the wok, oiled side-down, and brush the top with seasoning oil too. After 30 seconds, flip the pitta bread to toast the other side for 30 seconds. Repeat with the remaining pitta breads.

Mix together the sriracha and vegan mayonnaise in a small bowl.

To serve, place a patty inside each pitta bread pocket, dress with some shredded iceberg lettuce and drizzle over some sriracha vegan mayo. Serve immediately.

Blueberry & Lychee Buckwheat Pancakes

kcal — 390
carbs — 47.8g
protein — 8.7g
fat — 18.6g

Serves 4
(makes 4 small
pancakes)

10 min   10 min

I never tire of American-style pancakes; they are so good when topped with fresh fruit. I like to use buckwheat flour, but you can use any flour you prefer. The 'egg' substitute comes in the form of chia seeds, which, when combined with water, take on an 'eggy' consistency. The trick is not to over-beat the pancakes, as the batter can easily become too stiff. Simple and tasty – perfect for a Sunday brunch.

2 tbsp chia seeds

200g (7oz) buckwheat flour

2 tsp baking powder

½ tsp sea salt

1 tbsp rapeseed oil, plus extra for frying

1 tbsp golden caster sugar

200ml (7fl oz) coconut milk

handful of blueberries, plus extra to serve

handful of canned lychees, drained, roughly chopped, plus extra to serve

To serve

icing sugar, for dusting

3 squares dark chocolate, for grating

golden syrup, for drizzling

To make the chia 'egg', mix the chia seeds with 4 tbsp water in a small bowl. Let stand for 5 minutes before using.

Meanwhile, sift the flour and baking powder into a mixing bowl. Stir in the sea salt.

In a separate bowl, mix together the rapeseed oil and golden caster sugar. Add the coconut milk and chia 'egg' and mix together to combine.

Pour the wet ingredients into the dry mixture and stir gently to combine; do not over-mix.

Gently stir in the blueberries and lychees, then rest the batter for 5 minutes.

Heat a wok over a medium heat. Add a little rapeseed oil and swirl it around in the wok. Once hot, drop a spoonful of batter into the wok and cook for 2–3 minutes until bubbles start to appear. Flip and cook for 1 minute on the other side. Set aside and keep warm while you make the other pancakes.

To serve, dust the pancakes with icing sugar, top with more blueberries and lychees, grate over some dark chocolate and drizzle with golden syrup. Enjoy!

Red Bean & Lady Grey Tea Muffin

kcal — 367
carbs — 50.6g
protein — 6.1g
fat — 16.8g

Makes 4 muffins

10 min   35 min

These muffins are an exciting and interesting combination of Japanese adzuki red bean paste and Lady Grey tea. They are so simple to make and are the perfect weekend brunch treat!

2 Lady Grey tea bags

1 tbsp chia seeds

90g (3¼oz) unsalted sunflower spread, at room temperature

70g (2½oz) golden caster sugar

¼ tsp sea salt

70g (2½oz) sweetened adzuki red bean paste (from a tin)

1 tsp baking powder

120g (4¼oz) plain wholemeal flour

handful of rolled oats, to garnish

1 tbsp cooked adzuki beans, to garnish

Preheat the oven to 180°C/160°C fan/350°F/Gas Mark 4.

Pour 80ml (5½ tbsp) boiling water into a bowl or jug. Add the tea bags and leave to stand in the water for 5 minutes.

Remove the tea bags and set the tea aside for 10 minutes to cool.

To make a chia 'egg', mix the chia seeds with 2 tbsp water in a small bowl. Let stand for 5 minutes.

In a large bowl, beat together the sunflower spread and sugar until smooth and pale in colour. Add the sea salt and the adzuki red bean paste and beat well.

Slowly add the chia 'egg' to the mixture, stirring after each addition.

Sieve half the baking powder and half the flour into the mixture and mix well, then add half the tea and stir to combine.

Sieve in the remaining baking powder and flour and mix, followed by the remaining tea. Mix well.

Divide the mixture between four individual muffin cases in a muffin tin. Scatter some oats over the top and bake for 30–35 minutes.

Remove from the oven and allow to cool in their cases on a wire rack. Once cool, divide the cooked adzuki beans between the muffins, placing them in the centre of each muffin, then serve.

Tropical Overnight Oat Pots

kcal — 417
carbs — 61.9g
protein — 10.1g
fat — 14.0g

Serves 1

10 min
+
overnight

These overnight oat pots are quick, easy and full of nutrition. When I have guests staying over, it is so easy to prepare these the night before and serve along with an assortment of Asian tropical fruits, such as mangos, pineapples and papayas, as part of a continental breakfast. Just scale up the quantities depending on how many servings you need. So easy – and a great way to impress your guests!

4 tbsp rolled oats

2 tbsp chia seeds

200ml (7fl oz) coconut drink (I use Apro)

For the topping

3–4 mango slices

2 tbsp finely diced pineapple

1 tbsp golden syrup

toasted sesame seeds, for sprinkling

ground sunflower seeds or flaxseed, for sprinkling

sprig of fresh mint, to garnish

Pour the oats into a glass jar. Top with the chia seeds and add the coconut milk. Stir and place, covered, in the refrigerator.

The next morning, remove the pot from the refrigerator. Top with fresh mango and pineapple, drizzle over some golden syrup, sprinkle over toasted sesame seeds and your chosen ground seeds, then garnish with mint and serve.

Cleansing Ginger & Apple Cider Vinegar Drink

Serves 1

kcal — 45
carbs — 10.7g
protein — 0.2g
fat — 0.1g

3 min

This is a great cleansing drink to have before breakfast. I add agave or maple syrup and ginger for a powerful flu-busting remedy. Buy unfiltered organic apple cider vinegar that contains 'the mother', i.e. protein, enzymes and friendly bacteria.

1 tbsp freshly grated root ginger

1 tbsp unfiltered, naturally fermented apple cider vinegar with 'mother'

1 tbsp agave or maple syrup

Put all the ingredients in a heatproof glass or mug with 250ml (9fl oz) warm boiled water. Stir well and drink on an empty stomach. After drinking, wait 30 minutes before eating solid foods.

Goji Berry 'Tea'

Serves 1

kcal — 32
carbs — 5.9g
protein — 1.1g
fat — 0.2g

3 min

This Eastern remedy is very good for the eyes, because goji berries are a source of beta-carotene. Try it every day for three months – my uncle, who is in his sixties, has almost perfect vision! Healthy and good for you: what's not to love?

small handful of dried goji berries

Rinse the goji berries and place them in a heatproof glass. Pour in 500ml (18fl oz) boiling water and leave to steep until cool enough to drink. After drinking, wait 30 minutes before a meal.

'Super 10'
Juice/Smoothie

15 min

Serves 3

kcal — 88
carbs — 12.8g
protein — 5.8g
fat — 1.9g

This super healthy juice with 10 fresh ingredients is full of micronutrients and delicious either juiced or as a smoothie. With blending, you keep the fibre of the fruits and stay fuller for longer. Either way, the plant goodness will keep your cells buzzing.

2.5cm (1in) piece of fresh root ginger, peeled

small bunch of mint

½ lemon, peeled and sliced

100g (3½oz) baby spinach

50g (1¾oz) kale, sliced

30g (1oz) broccoli florets

1 cucumber, halved lengthways

1 small carrot, sliced

150g (5½oz) celery stalks

2 gala apples, cored and roughly chopped

1 tbsp ground spirulina

If you're making a smoothie, put all the fresh ingredients into a blender and blend. If you're making a juice, put all the fresh ingredients into a juicer and juice.

To serve, pour into glasses, add the spirulina and stir to mix well. It's best to drink this immediately for all the goodness. If you like, you can pour it into a glass jar with an airtight lid, keep it refrigerated and drink throughout the day.

Avocado, Spinach,
Nut & Date Shake

5 min

Serves 1

kcal — 293
carbs — 18.8g
protein — 10.5g
fat — 19.4g

This green, sweet, nutty avocado shake is packed full of goodness. The spinach provides folic acid and the dates add a toffee-caramel sweetness. It will satisfy the taste buds while giving your immune system a boost! Enjoy.

½ avocado, peeled, stoned and sliced

100g (3½oz) baby spinach

1 tsp raw cashew nuts, pine nuts or almonds

1 tsp ground flaxseed

1 tbsp ground spirulina

200ml (7fl oz) coconut drink (I use Apro)

2 dates

Simply put all the ingredients into a blender and blend until smooth. Drink immediately.

Papaya & Almond Milk Smoothie

Serves 1

kcal — 212
carbs — 35.4g
protein — 3.5g
fat — 7.3g

This sweet-tasting 'milk' is great on its own for a light breakfast. The riper the papaya, the more 'honey sweet' it is. I've used almond milk here, but you can use whatever dairy-free milk you prefer.

½ small papaya, deseeded, peeled and sliced into chunks

300ml (10fl oz) almond milk

½ tsp ground turmeric

1 tbsp golden syrup, or agave or maple syrup (optional)

5 toasted almonds

Place all the ingredients into a blender and blitz to form a smoothie. Pour out into a glass and serve immediately.

Hakka Lei Latte

Serves 1

kcal — 396
carbs — 31.4g
protein — 10.6g
fat — 25.7g

This shake is inspired by a tea made by the Hakka tribe in Taiwan, China, who taught me how to make their nutty, healthy drink in 2006. The pumpkin seeds contain zinc and omega-3 and -6 fatty acids, meaning this drink is rich in both taste and nutrition.

1 tsp each white sesame seeds and black sesame seeds

1 tbsp each pumpkin seeds and sunflower seeds

1 tsp freshly grated root ginger

½ tsp matcha green tea powder

1 tbsp cashew butter

1 tbsp golden syrup

250ml (9fl oz) nut milk of your choice

Using a pestle and mortar, crush the white and black sesame seeds, pumpkin seeds and sunflower seeds, then transfer to a mug. Add the ginger, matcha green tea powder, cashew butter and golden syrup.

Pour your chosen nut milk into a wok or saucepan and bring to a simmer over a low heat. Pour into the mug and use a small whisk to mix everything together well. Drink immediately.

2.

Nourishing
Soups

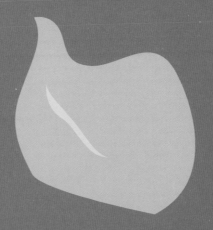

Nourishing Shiitake, Miso, Spinach & Tofu Soup

Serves 2 as a main or 4 as a starter

kcal — 150
carbs — 6.7g
protein — 14.8g
fat — 6.4g

This broth is so quick to prepare and makes a comforting and nutritious dinner. It can be served as a starter or as a main if you're after something light. If you have a larger appetite, add some soybean noodles (or ramen noodles of your choice) at the end to make this more substantial.

3 tbsp red miso paste

2.5cm (1in) piece of fresh root ginger, grated

½ tsp vegetable bouillon powder

200g (7oz) fresh shiitake mushrooms, sliced

200g (7oz) fresh, firm tofu, cut into 1cm (½in) cubes

100g (3½oz) baby spinach leaves

3 large spring onions, trimmed and sliced into 1cm (½in) rounds, to garnish

Pour 800ml (1½ pints) water into a saucepan or wok over a high heat and bring to the boil. Reduce the heat to medium to bring to a simmer.

Add the miso, ginger and bouillon powder. Stir well to dissolve the miso and bouillon.

Add the shiitake mushrooms and tofu. Cook gently for 10 minutes.

Finally, add the spinach and stir until it wilts. Serve immediately, topped with the spring onions.

Korean-style Seaweed Soup

Serves 4 as a starter

kcal — 46
carbs — 1.6g
protein — 2.4g
fat — 3.4g

This is my version of a soup I first had in a small Korean restaurant in Hong Kong run by two Korean women. It was the perfect soul food – a soothing, light and nutritious supper. You can add tofu cubes if you want to up your protein intake. The seaweed provides that slightly umami taste of the sea.

400ml (14fl oz) vegetable stock

small handful of dried wakame seaweed

1 tbsp doenjang

7 dried nori sheets, torn into bite-sized pieces

2 spring onions, trimmed and finely sliced

pinch of sea salt

1 tbsp toasted sesame oil

Place all the ingredients in a wok or medium saucepan over a medium heat and add 400ml (14fl oz) water.

Bring to a simmer, then cook for 8 minutes.

Divide between four bowls and serve immediately.

Mama Huang's Onion, Tomato & Enoki Soup

Serves 2

kcal — 72
carbs — 10.0g
protein — 2.8g
fat — 2.5g

My mum is a brilliantly inventive cook. When she came to stay with us in 2018, she whipped up this magical soup from odds and ends and it has been a firm favourite ever since. The onion and tomatoes develop a sweetness as you simmer them.

1 onion, roughly chopped

5 large, fresh tomatoes, roughly chopped

pinch of sea salt

pinch of ground white pepper, plus extra to taste

1 tbsp vegetable bouillon powder

200g (7oz) fresh enoki mushrooms, trimmed and sliced into 1cm (½in) slices

toasted sesame oil, to season

5g (1/8oz) fresh chives, finely chopped, to garnish

Put the onion, tomatoes, salt, white pepper and bouillon into a food processor and blitz to a fine liquid.

Pour the mixture into a wok or medium-sized saucepan over a medium heat and add 300ml (10fl oz) water. Bring to a simmer, then cook for 10 minutes.

Stir in the enoki mushrooms and cook for 2 minutes until just wilted. Season to taste with toasted sesame oil and ground white pepper.

Serve garnished with finely chopped chives for a fresh, oniony bite.

Grandma's Golden Needle, Carrot & Daikon Soup

Serves 2 or 4 as a starter

kcal — 162
carbs — 17.3g
protein — 6.3g
fat — 8.2g

Whenever I think of golden needles, I think of my maternal grandmother. She would often pair them with pork ribs or meaty dried shiitake mushrooms. Golden needles are a delicate Chinese vegetable with a sweet, carroty taste.

1 tbsp rapeseed oil

2.5cm (1in) piece of fresh root ginger, sliced into rounds

1 small carrot, diced into 0.5cm (¼in) cubes

½ daikon, peeled and diced into 0.5cm (¼in) cubes

2 tomatoes, hard centres discarded, finely chopped

1 tbsp vegetable bouillon powder

40g (1½oz) dried golden needles, pre-soaked in warm water for 10 minutes (or dried shiitake mushrooms or tinned bamboo shoots, sliced into julienne strips)

1 tbsp tamari or low-sodium light soy sauce

1 tsp toasted sesame oil

pinch of ground white pepper

Heat a wok over a medium heat and add the rapeseed oil. Once hot, add the ginger and stir for a few seconds, then add the carrot, daikon and tomatoes and toss for a few seconds.

Add 700ml (1¼ pints) water along with the bouillon powder and give it all a good stir. Bring to a simmer and cook for 10 minutes.

Reduce the heat to low. Stir in the golden needles and cook, gently, for 2 minutes. Season with the tamari or light soy sauce, toasted sesame oil and ground white pepper and serve immediately.

Chinese Sweetcorn Soup with Black Truffle

kcal — 247
carbs — 32.9g
protein — 6.8g
fat — 10.5g

Serves 2

10 min   10 min

Who doesn't love sweetcorn soup? This soup brings out my inner child. The chunky sweetcorn kernels are so satisfying, but I like to add shavings of black truffle for a nutty, rich and decadent treat. If you are a die-hard vegan, then omit the truffle. Truffles are a fungus, but sometimes pigs are used to sniff for them. Whether or not you agree with this depends on your own personal stance. Truffle or no truffle, this Chinese-style sweetcorn soup never fails to hit the spot.

1 large tbsp cornflour

1 tbsp rapeseed oil

2.5cm (1in) piece of fresh root ginger, grated

340g (12oz) can sweetcorn, drained

100g (3½oz) cherry tomatoes, halved

1 tsp vegetable bouillon powder

1 tbsp Shaohsing rice wine or dry sherry

8 fresh shiitake mushrooms, sliced

1 tbsp tamari or low-sodium light soy sauce

1 tsp toasted sesame oil

pinch of sea salt

pinch of ground white pepper

2 spring onions, trimmed and finely sliced into rounds

shavings of black truffle (optional), to garnish

In a small bowl, mix the cornflour with 2 tbsp cold water to form a slurry. Set aside until needed.

Heat a wok over a high heat and add the rapeseed oil. Once hot, add the ginger and stir-fry for a few seconds, then add the sweetcorn, cherry tomatoes, bouillon powder and rice wine or sherry, along with 600ml (20fl oz) water. Bring to the boil, then add the fresh shiitake mushrooms and cook for 2 minutes.

Season with the tamari or light soy sauce, toasted sesame oil, salt and ground white pepper. Pour in the cornflour slurry and stir gently to thicken. Add the spring onions and give the soup one final stir.

Divide between two bowls. If using truffles, grate generously over each bowl, then serve immediately.

Smoked Tofu Dumplings in Hot & Sour Broth

kcal — 200
carbs — 25.5g
protein — 13.1g
fat — 6.3g

Serves 2
(makes 10 dumplings)

30 min   5 min

I am addicted to the flavour combination of hot and sour. This soup is another version, this time with my vegan dumplings as the star. The broth is inspired by Cantonese hot and sour soup – the use of dark soy and Chinkiang black rice vinegar make for a sour-umami hit. The trick to making flavourful veggie dumplings is to marinate the tofu in mushroom sauce to achieve a richer flavour.

For the dumplings

50g (1¾oz) smoked tofu, drained, rinsed in cold water and cubed

40g (1½oz) firm tofu, crumbled

60g (2¼oz) long-stem broccoli, stems finely chopped

2.5cm (1in) piece of fresh root ginger, grated

1 spring onion, trimmed and finely chopped

¼ tsp salt

¼ vegetable stock cube, grated

¼ tsp golden caster sugar

¼ tsp white pepper

½ tsp pure sesame oil

½ tsp sea salt

1 tbsp vegetarian mushroom stir-fry sauce

10 sheets shop-bought dumpling skins

For the hot & sour broth

700ml (1¼ pints) vegetable stock

100g (3½oz) oyster mushrooms, whole

50g (1¾oz) French beans, sliced on a deep angle

2 tbsp tamari or low-sodium light soy sauce

1 tsp dark soy sauce

1 tbsp Chinkiang black rice vinegar

large pinch of ground white pepper

½ red chilli, sliced

To garnish

spring onion slices, red chilli julienne strips, coriander leaves

Place both kinds of tofu in a bowl along with the broccoli florets and stems, grated ginger and spring onion. Mix thoroughly until well combined.

Add the rest of the dumpling ingredients (except the skins) and mix well.

Place a dumpling skin on your palm. Place 2 generous tsp of the vegetable mixture in the middle of the skin. Dip your finger in water and run it around the edges of the dumpling to wet them. Fold one half over the other and press the edges together to seal. If you want to make the dumpling more decorative, fold the ends. Repeat with the remaining dumpling skins and mixture.

Place a large saucepan over a high heat. Add all the ingredients for the broth and bring to the boil.

Half-fill another saucepan with water and bring to the boil. Gently drop all the dumplings into the boiling water. Let the dumplings cook, stirring occasionally to prevent sticking. The dumplings are cooked when they all float up to the surface (about 2–3 minutes).

Remove the dumplings from the pan using a slotted spoon and transfer them to the serving bowls (see tip).

Ladle over the hot and sour broth to cover the dumplings. Garnish with finely chopped spring onions, red chillies and coriander and serve immediately.

Ching's Tip — You can also eat the dumplings as they are once you've cooked them. They are known as *shui jiao* ('water cooked'). Serve with your favourite dipping sauce.

Button Mushroom
Tom Yum

kcal — 118
carbs — 17.6g
protein — 6.4g
fat — 2.6g

Serves 2 or 4 as a starter

10 min   12 min

This is another 'hot and sour' soup, but hailing from a different part of the world – Thailand! It's one of my favourites. Filled with fresh vegetables and herbs, it is pungent, aromatic and addictively good. The button mushrooms absorb the flavours of the broth and deliver great satisfaction when you bite into them. I hope you enjoy it.

2.5cm (1in) piece of galangal or fresh root ginger, peeled

1 bunch of coriander, stalks and leaves separated

2 lemongrass stalks, sliced into 2.5cm (1in) pieces

1 tbsp vegetable bouillon powder

1 red chilli, deseeded and sliced

8 cherry tomatoes, halved

1 tsp tamarind paste

juice of 1 lime

3 kaffir lime leaves

large pinch of sea salt

200g (7oz) button mushrooms, quartered

225g (8oz) can bamboo shoots, rinsed, drained and sliced

100g (3½oz) pea aubergines, (optional)

1 sweetcorn cob, sliced into 4 x 1.5cm (¾in) rounds

1–2 tsp golden caster sugar

1 tbsp clear rice vinegar

Use a pestle and mortar to bruise the galangal or ginger, the coriander stalks and the lemongrass, then set aside.

Heat a wok over a high heat and add 1 litre (1¾ pints) water. Stir in the vegetable bouillon powder, then add the galangal or ginger, coriander stalks, lemongrass, chilli, tomatoes, tamarind paste, lime juice and kaffir lime leaves and bring to simmer. Season with sea salt and cook for 4 minutes.

Add the button mushrooms, bamboo shoots, pea aubergines (if using) and the sweetcorn. Cook for 1–2 minutes. Add the caster sugar to taste and season with the clear rice vinegar. Transfer to bowls and garnish with the coriander leaves. Serve immediately.

Hot & Sour Soup

kcal — 194
carbs — 20.0g
protein — 9.3g
fat — 8.8g

Serves 4

15 min   10 min

I was taught this comforting soup recipe by Mama Huang, the ultimate queen of hot and sour soup. It is clear and uses daikon and enoki mushrooms for a slightly sweet taste. The 'hot' comes from the ginger, chilli and white pepper, and the 'sour' relies on using rice vinegar for a delicious tang, while the pungent daikon and fresh coriander create a distinctive aroma. To turn it into a noodle soup, simply add cooked vermicelli rice noodles at the end.

50g (1¾oz) dried wood ear mushrooms

1 tbsp cornflour

1 tbsp rapeseed oil

2.5cm (1in) piece of fresh root ginger, grated

1 red chilli, deseeded and finely chopped

8 cherry tomatoes, left whole

3 leaves of Chinese leaf, finely sliced

1 carrot, sliced into julienne strips

1 daikon, peeled and sliced into julienne strips

225g (8oz) can bamboo shoots, rinsed, drained and sliced into julienne strips

1 tbsp vegetable bouillon powder

2 tbsp tamari or low-sodium light soy sauce

2 tbsp clear rice vinegar

1 tbsp toasted sesame oil

200g (7oz) fresh, firm tofu, drained and sliced into julienne strips

200g (7oz) enoki mushrooms, separated into smaller bunches and ends trimmed

3 spring onions, trimmed and sliced into julienne strips

small handful of coriander, stalks finely sliced and leaves set aside for garnish

large pinch of ground white pepper

Before you begin, place the wood ear mushrooms in a bowl. Pour over boiling water and leave to soak for 20 minutes, then drain. Slice the mushrooms into julienne strips.

In a small bowl, mix the cornflour with 2 tbsp cold water to form a slurry. Set aside until needed.

Heat a wok over a high heat and add the rapeseed oil. Once hot, add the ginger and chilli and stir for a few seconds, then add the tomatoes and toss for a few seconds more.

Add the Chinese leaves, carrot, daikon, bamboo shoots and bouillon powder, then pour over 1 litre (1¾ pints) water.

Bring to the boil, then reduce the heat to medium and simmer for 5 minutes until the Chinese leaves are translucent. Add the wood ear mushrooms and cook for 1 minute, then add the tamari or light soy sauce, rice vinegar and toasted sesame oil. Pour in the cornflour slurry to thicken.

Stir in the tofu and enoki mushrooms and cook for 1 minute, then add the spring onions and coriander stalks. Season with ground white pepper.

Spoon out into serving bowls. Garnish with the coriander leaves and eat immediately.

Ching's Tip — After you have sliced your spring onions into julienne strips, plunge them into iced water to make beautiful spring onion curls.

3.

Fresh & Exotic Salads

Bang Bang Shiitake Mushrooms Salad

kcal — 270
carbs — 27.3g
protein — 4.2g
fat — 16.2g

Serves 4

15 min   2–3min

This noodle salad originated in Sichuan as a street-food dish that could be whipped up in minutes. 'Bang bang' comes from the Mandarin word for 'stick', as a stick was traditionally used to either pound chicken or flatten dough to make wheat-flour noodles. My plant-based version of the dish uses the fibrous stalks of shiitake mushrooms, which can be 'shredded' in much the same way as chicken. It is tasty and nutritious and works great as a meat-free alternative. For an even speedier supper, buy ready-to-eat vermicelli rice noodles from the supermarket.

100g (3½oz) vermicelli mung bean noodles or ready-to-eat vermicelli rice noodles

1 tbsp rapeseed oil

300g (10½oz) shiitake mushrooms, stalks shredded and tops sliced into julienne strips

pinch of Chinese five spice

2 tbsp tamari or low-sodium light soy sauce

½ cucumber, sliced into julienne strips

1 large carrot, sliced into julienne strips

100g (3½oz) radishes, sliced into mini matchsticks

1 large spring onion, trimmed and sliced into julienne strips

2 tbsp black sesame seeds, to garnish

For the dressing

2 tbsp rapeseed oil

2.5cm (1in) piece of fresh root ginger, finely grated

1 red chilli, deseeded and finely chopped

½ tsp toasted ground Sichuan pepper

½ tsp dried chilli flakes

1 tbsp toasted sesame oil

1 tsp tahini

1 tsp crunchy peanut butter

1 tbsp tamari or low-sodium light soy sauce

2 tbsp Chinkiang black rice vinegar

If you are using mung bean vermicelli rice noodles, soak them in hot water for 10 minutes, then drain.

Heat a wok over a high heat until smoking, and add the rapeseed oil. Once hot, add the mushrooms, season with the Chinese five spice and toss for 2 seconds. Add the tamari or light soy sauce and stir-fry for 1 minute, then take off the heat.

Add all the dressing ingredients to a jar. Put the lid on and shake well, then set aside.

To serve, divide the noodles between plates, then top with the cucumber, carrot, radishes and spring onion. Top with the shredded mushrooms and pour over the nutty dressing. Garnish with black sesame seeds and serve immediately. To enjoy at its best, mix it all together well.

Xian Chinese-inspired 'Kachumber'

kcal — 164
carbs — 16.0g
protein — 6.4g
fat — 9.1g

Serves 4

15 min   30 sec

Kachumber is an Indian salad made with cumin, shallots, radishes, tomatoes and cucumbers. I often make my own Xian-style version of it at home, adding chickpeas, kohlrabi and different spices. It's easy to prepare in advance and is great served with some toasted sourdough and dairy-free yogurt as a light snack. If you cannot get kolhrabi, just leave it out. The crunchy textures and aromatic spices make this dish so satisfying and addictive to eat.

1 small red onion, finely diced

10 cherry tomatoes, halved

1 cucumber, deseeded and diced into 1cm (½in) cubes

1 carrot, diced into 1cm (½in) cubes

6 red radishes, trimmed and diced into 1cm (½in) cubes

1 kohlrabi, peeled and diced into 1cm (½in) cubes

400g (14oz) can chickpeas, drained and rinsed well

dairy-free yogurt, to serve

toasted pumpkin seeds, to garnish

For the spice mix

½ tsp each cumin seeds, fennel seeds, dried chilli flakes and ground turmeric

2 large pinches of sea salt

For the dressing

2 tbsp olive oil

juice of 2 lemons

pinch of soft brown sugar

In a wok or small pan, dry toast the spice mix over a medium heat for 30 seconds until fragrant. Once toasted, transfer to a spice grinder or pestle and mortar and grind well, then set aside.

In a large bowl, mix together the onion, cherry tomatoes, cucumber, carrot, radishes, kohlrabi and chickpeas.

Make the dressing by putting the olive oil, lemon juice and sugar into a jar. Add the toasted, ground spices, then put the lid on and shake well to combine. Pour the dressing over the salad, reserving 1 tbsp. If you want to serve the salad later, you can transfer it to the refrigerator at this point.

When you're ready to eat, top the kachumber with a dollop of dairy-free yogurt. Drizzle the reserved dressing over the yogurt, then sprinkle over the toasted pumpkin seeds and eat immediately with some toasted sourdough bread.

Hunan-style Crispy Sweet Chilli Mushroom & Noodle Salad

kcal — 490
carbs — 90.9g
protein — 16.3g
fat — 8.8g

Serves 2 as a starter
or a light main meal

10 min   15 min

The people of the Hunan region in China are known for their love of sweet and spicy combinations. This easy dish is inspired by these strong flavour profiles. Save time by buying ready-to-eat vermicelli rice noodles. This recipe calls for aquafaba: this is the beige liquid found in tinned chickpeas. It acts as a thickening agent and egg substitute, making it perfect for panko-ing the mushrooms to give them a crispy texture.

For the mushrooms

500g (1lb 2oz) shimeji mushrooms, separated

pinch of sea salt

pinch of ground white pepper

pinch of Chinese five spice

2 tbsp potato flour or cornflour

3 tbsp aquafaba

100g (3½oz) vegan panko breadcrumbs

6 sprays of low-calorie olive oil

For the sauce

1 tsp rapeseed oil

2.5cm (1in) piece of fresh root ginger, finely grated

4 long, dried chillies

1 tbsp tamari or low-sodium light soy sauce

2 tbsp sweet chilli sauce

juice and zest of 1 large orange

For the salad

1 head of romaine lettuce leaves, shredded

½ cucumber, cut into half-moon slices

1 large carrot, cut into fine matchsticks

200g (7oz) ready-to-eat vermicelli rice noodles

1 tbsp sesame seeds, toasted

spring onion curls, to serve (see tip on page 42)

Preheat the oven to 200°C/180°C fan/400°F/Gas Mark 6.

Lay the mushrooms on a roasting tray and season with the salt, pepper and Chinese five spice.

Place the flour, aquafaba and panko breadcrumbs in three separate dishes. One at a time, dip each mushroom into the flour, covering and coating well, then into the aquafaba, and finally quickly dip into the breadcrumbs. Once coated, return to the roasting tray and repeat with the remaining mushrooms. Spray the mushrooms with olive oil, then roast in the oven for 15 minutes until crispy.

Meanwhile, heat a wok over a high heat until smoking. Once hot, add the rapeseed oil, then add the ginger and stir-fry for a few seconds. Next add the chillies, tamari or soy sauce, sweet chilli sauce, and orange zest and juice. Bring to the boil and reduce until thickened.

When the mushrooms are ready, remove them from the oven. Drizzle the sauce over the crispy mushrooms and toss to coat.

Serve the mushrooms on a bed of lettuce, cucumber, carrot and rice noodles. Drizzle over more of the sauce if you like. Sprinkle over the toasted sesame seeds and top with spring onion curls. Serve immediately.

Japanese Tofu, Mushroom & Pickle Hand Rolls

kcal — 478
carbs — 70.4g
protein — 21.4g
fat — 13.7g

Serves 4

10 min   30 min

I love Japanese-style sushi hand rolls. Not only are they great for a healthy, light supper, they are also so fun to assemble and eat. I think this is a much more forgiving and fuss-free way of enjoying sushi, rather than worrying about how to create perfect rolls. My simple, Japanese-inspired dish is also perfect for entertaining and children's parties, as everyone can roll and make their own – it's the perfect sharing dish!

300g (10½oz) brown rice

600ml (20fl oz) vegetable stock

1 tbsp rapeseed oil

400g (14oz) firm tofu, drained and sliced into 2cm (¾in) batons

200g (7oz) enoki mushrooms or fresh sliced shiitake mushrooms

1 tbsp Shaohsing rice wine or dry sherry

1 tsp dark soy sauce

2 tbsp tamari or low-sodium light soy sauce

1 tbsp clear rice vinegar

pinch of shichimi togarashi pepper flakes

1 tbsp toasted sesame oil

small handful of finely sliced chives

2 small handfuls baby spinach leaves

1 pack of 8 sushi nori sheets, sliced in half on the diagonal to create 16 triangular pieces

For the pickled veg

1 cucumber, deseeded and sliced into julienne strips

1 carrot, sliced into julienne strips

1 red and 1 yellow pepper, sliced into julienne strips

1 tsp black sesame seeds

100ml (3½fl oz) seasoned sushi rice vinegar

To serve

sriracha, pickled sushi ginger and pickled yellow daikon

To make the pickled veg, place all the ingredients in a non-metallic dish. Cover and chill in the refrigerator for 20 minutes.

Meanwhile, rinse the rice well, making sure the water runs clear. Place the rice and vegetable stock in a medium saucepan over a high heat and bring to the boil. Reduce the heat to low, cover the pan with a tight-fitting lid and let the rice cook for 20 minutes. Once the rice is cooked, fluff up the grains and transfer to a shallow dish to cool.

Heat a wok over a high heat until smoking, and add the rapeseed oil. Once hot, add the tofu and mushrooms and let them sit in the wok for 2 minutes, then deglaze the wok with the Shaohsing rice wine or sherry. Add the dark soy sauce, tamari or light soy sauce and clear rice vinegar and toss, loosening the tofu carefully. Season with the shichimi togarashi pepper flakes and the toasted sesame oil and stir. Sprinkle over the finely sliced chives, then transfer the mixture to a serving plate.

Remove the pickle from the refrigerator and transfer to a serving bowl.

Set out the spinach leaves, nori, rice, mushroom tofu mixture and pickled vegetables. To roll, take a piece of nori and fill it with some rice, some pickle, some tofu and mushrooms and a few spinach leaves. Roll it up to eat and serve with the sriracha, sushi ginger and pickled daikon on the side for dipping.

Gochujang Spinach, Gem Lettuce & Radish Salad

kcal — 122
carbs — 12.3g
protein — 4.1g
fat — 6.6g

Serves 2 as a side

15 min

This easy side salad is a heady mix of spicy, sweet, tangy, fresh flavours. It also makes a perfect accompaniment to other light meals in the summer months. Add smoked tofu cubes to turn this into a light dinner, or simply add roasted shiitake mushrooms.

½ red onion, thinly sliced into half-moon slices

100g (3½oz) cherry tomatoes, halved

200g (7oz) radishes, trimmed and sliced into rounds

100g (3½oz) baby spinach leaves

100g (3½oz) little gem lettuce leaves, separated

For the dressing

1 garlic clove, minced

1 tbsp gochujang chilli paste

1 tbsp toasted sesame oil

2 tbsp clear rice vinegar

a pinch of caster sugar

Place the onion, cherry tomatoes, radishes, spinach leaves and lettuce leaves in a salad bowl and toss to combine.

In a pestle and mortar, grind the garlic, gochujang chilli paste, sesame oil, rice vinegar and sugar and mix well to combine. Pour the dressing over the salad, massaging it into the salad leaves. Serve immediately as a side salad.

Radish, Cucumber &
Wood Ear Mushroom 'Pickle'

Serves 2 or 4
as a starter

30 min

This is a fresh, quick 'pickle' salad that I love serving as a light supper in summer. It's perfect with plain jasmine rice and a dollop of chilli sauce on the side, and makes a simple, light meal for when I have overindulged! The wood ear mushrooms add a delightfully crunchy texture.

50g (1¾oz) shredded dried Chinese wood ear mushrooms

1 garlic clove, finely chopped

2.5cm (1in) piece of fresh root ginger, finely chopped

2 spring onions, trimmed and finely chopped

100g (3½oz) radishes, trimmed and finely sliced

½ cucumber, sliced into julienne strips

2 tbsp tamari or low-sodium light soy sauce

2 tbsp clear rice vinegar

½ tsp chilli bean paste

1 tbsp toasted sesame oil

1 tsp chilli oil

small handful of coriander, finely chopped

cooked jasmine rice, to serve (see page 194)

Before you begin, soaked the dried mushrooms in warm water for 20 minutes, then drain.

In a small food processor, mince the garlic, ginger and spring onions. Transfer to a bowl and add the drained mushrooms, along with the radishes and cucumber. Add the tamari or soy sauce, rice vinegar, chilli bean paste, sesame oil and chilli oil and stir to combine. Chill in the refrigerator for 15 minutes.

When you're ready to serve, add the coriander, toss everything together and serve immediately with jasmine rice.

Wok-fried Orange-Soy Sticky Sprouts & Wild Rice Salad

kcal — 488
carbs — 75.6g
protein — 19.9g
fat — 14.7g

Serves 2

20 min   6 min

Brussels sprouts are full of antioxidants and you just know they are doing you the world of good! Here I wok-fry them until sticky and serve them on a bed of wild rice with chicory leaves and smoked tofu cubes, topped with finely chopped dried sweet cranberries for the perfect satisfying and nourishing salad.

200g (7oz) Brussels sprouts, trimmed

pinch of salt

1 tbsp rapeseed oil

2.5cm (1in) piece of fresh root ginger, grated

juice of 1 orange

50ml (2fl oz) vegetable stock

1 tbsp hoisin sauce

1 tbsp golden syrup

1 tbsp tamari or low-sodium light soy sauce

1 tsp dark soy sauce

1 tbsp toasted flaked almonds, to serve

juice and zest of 1 lemon, to serve

For the salad

100g (3½oz) smoked tofu, drained, rinsed in cold water and sliced into 0.5cm (¼in) cubes

2 heads of chicory, washed, leaves separated

1 small handful of dried cranberries, finely chopped

150g (5½oz) cooked wild rice, cooled

150g (5½oz) cooked jasmine rice, cooled (see page 194)

1 red chilli, deseeded and finely chopped

1 spring onion, trimmed and finely sliced

In a wok or medium saucepan, bring 500ml (18fl oz) water to the boil over a medium heat. Add the Brussels sprouts and salt and boil for 4 minutes. Drain and refresh under cold water, then set aside.

Place all the salad ingredients in a large bowl and mix well. Cover and leave to chill in the refrigerator.

Heat a wok over a high heat until smoking, and add the rapeseed oil. Once hot, add the ginger, orange juice, vegetable stock, hoisin sauce, golden syrup, tamari or light soy sauce and dark soy sauce. Bring to the bubble, then reduce to a sticky glaze. Add the cooked Brussels sprouts and toss together, coating well.

To serve, spoon some of the salad mixture on to a plate. Top with the hot, sticky sprouts and garnish with some toasted flaked almonds. Squeeze over some lemon juice, sprinkle over the lemon zest, and eat immediately.

'Pure Health 12' Salad

kcal — 341
carbs — 37.7g
protein — 14.8g
fat — 15.5g

Serves 4 as a side

15 min

In this healthy salad, the ingredients speak for themselves. This is a chance to get an amazing variety of fruit and vegetables all in one hit. Using wholegrain mustard in the salad dressing gives a peppery note and enhances the umami flavours, making this an incredibly addictive, rich-tasting fresh salad. This makes the perfect centrepiece for family buffets and gatherings.

1 head of romaine lettuce, stalk removed, shredded

400g (14oz) can chickpeas, drained and rinsed

1 mango, peeled and finely diced

340g (12oz) can sweetcorn, drained

100g (3½oz) radishes, trimmed and sliced

100g (3½oz) cauliflower florets

10 cherry tomatoes, halved

1 avocado, peeled, stoned and sliced

100g (3½oz) cucumber, sliced into half-moon slices

100g (3½oz) carrot, peeled into fine curls with a potato peeler

3 celery sticks, finely sliced

100g (3½oz) hijiki seaweed or wakame seaweed (soaked in warm water for 10 minutes, then drained and rinsed)

watercress leaves, to garnish

For the dressing

1 tbsp extra virgin flaxseed oil

3 tbsp tamari or low-sodium light soy sauce

3 tbsp brown rice vinegar

1 tsp toasted sesame oil

1 tbsp wholegrain mustard

1 tbsp maple or agave syrup

Line the base of a large serving bowl with the romaine lettuce. Then arrange each of the ingredients in its own 'slice' or segment in the bowl, finally placing the seaweed in the centre. Garnish with watercress leaves.

Place all the dressing ingredients in a jar and shake. Place in a jug and serve with the salad.

Ginger Sesame
Soy Daikon

Serves 2

5 min
(20–25 if
soaking)

I love the peppery heat of raw daikon; this Asian radish is so cleansing and good for the gut. I like to simply serve it spiralised, in a ginger-sesame-soy dressing, garnished with baby spinach leaves and spring onions. To take the heat out of the daikon, you can soak it before using. This is a super delish dish, and is great as a side or as a light meal on its own. If you are not a fan of daikon, you can substitute with spiralised courgette.

1 daikon, trimmed, peeled and spiralised

1 tbsp clear rice vinegar (optional)

200g (7oz) baby spinach leaves

2 spring onions, trimmed and finely sliced into rounds, to garnish

toasted white sesame seeds, to garnish

For the dressing

1 tbsp freshly grated root ginger

1 tbsp tahini

2 tbsp tamari or low-sodium light soy sauce

1 tbsp toasted sesame oil

1 tbsp clear rice vinegar

1 tbsp golden syrup

For a less peppery heat, place the spiralised daikon in a bowl. Then cover with water, add 1 tbsp clear rice vinegar, and leave for 15–20 minutes. Drain and set aside.

Place all the dressing ingredients in a jar. Put on the lid and shake well to combine.

To serve, lay out the baby spinach leaves in a serving bowl. Top with the spiralised daikon, then drizzle over the creamy dressing. Scatter over the spring onions and toasted sesame seeds and eat immediately.

Miso-roasted Cauliflower with Chickpea, Carrot & Noodle Salad

kcal — 614
carbs — 70.3g
protein — 22.7g
fat — 29.0g

Serves 2 or 4 as a side

15 min

15–20 min

With Japanese miso and Middle Eastern tahini, this is such an 'East meets East'-inspired salad. The miso, garlic and soy dressing used to season the cauliflower delivers a rich umami hit as it roasts in the oven, while the accompanying noodle salad delivers on protein and fresh carroty sweetness. It's a match made in heaven, and a real crowd-pleaser.

1 large head of cauliflower

1 tbsp rapeseed oil

pinch of sea salt

pinch of freshly ground black pepper

2 garlic cloves, finely chopped

1 tbsp red miso paste

2 tbsp tamari or low-sodium light soy sauce

1 tbsp golden syrup

For the salad

400g (14oz) can chickpeas, drained and rinsed

2 carrots, sliced into julienne strips

200g (7oz) cooked vermicelli rice noodles

1 tbsp roasted cashew nuts

2 spring onions, trimmed and finely diced

For the dressing

1 tbsp each freshly grated root ginger, tahini, tamari or low-sodium light soy sauce, toasted sesame oil, rapeseed oil and clear rice vinegar

Preheat the oven to 180°C/160°C fan/350°F/Gas Mark 4.

Prepare the cauliflower. Discard the outer leaves, but keep the inner leaves and set aside. Break the cauliflower up into florets and place them in a roasting tray with the inner leaves. Season with the salt and pepper, and drizzle over the rapeseed oil.

Put the garlic, miso paste, tamari or light soy sauce and golden syrup in a jar and shake well to combine. Drizzle this mixture over the cauliflower florets and leaves, making sure they're well covered. Roast for 15–20 minutes.

Meanwhile, prepare the salad. Layer the chickpeas, carrots and noodles on a large platter. Place all the dressing ingredients in a jar and shake well, then set aside.

Remove the cauliflower from the oven and transfer it to the serving platter on top of the chickpea salad. Drizzle over the dressing, sprinkle over the cashew nuts and spring onions, and serve immediately.

California East Salad

kcal — 235
carbs — 12.0g
protein — 3.0g
fat — 19.8g

Serves 4 as a side

15 min

When my husband and I lived in LA, we loved visiting the farmers' markets. During the summer months, we often looked forward to buying assorted heirloom tomatoes, sweet, ripe nectarines and tender, white-fleshed peaches. This is one of my favourite salads to make, combining creamy avocado, sweet nectarines and peaches, sweet–sour tomatoes and peppery basil with umami-rich tamari, lemon juice and ginger.

100g (3½oz) assorted heirloom tomatoes, sliced into rounds

2 soft white-fleshed peaches, stoned and sliced into segments

2 soft yellow-fleshed nectarines or peaches, stoned and sliced into segments

2 ripe avocadoes, peeled, stoned and sliced

large handful basil leaves

pinch of sea salt

pinch of freshly ground black pepper

For the dressing

1 tbsp tamari or low-sodium light soy sauce

2 tbsp extra virgin olive oil

juice of ½ lemon

½ tsp golden caster sugar

1 tsp freshly grated root ginger

Arrange the heirloom tomatoes, peach and nectarine segments and avocado slices on a large serving plate as follows: one slice of tomato, followed by a slice of white-fleshed peach, then a slice of nectarine or yellow-fleshed peach, then a slice of avocado. Separate it from the next set of slices with basil leaves, then repeat until the platter is full and all the slices are used up. Sprinkle over the salt and pepper.

Combine the ingredients for the dressing in a large jar and shake well. To serve, drizzle the dressing over the salad and serve immediately.

Grilled Miso Corn with Red Cabbage

kcal — 195
carbs — 13.5g
protein — 5.5g
fat — 13.4g

Serves 4 as a side

15 min

3–5min

This is a tasty, versatile salad, perfect for the summer months. I just love the sweetness of the corn against the peppery bite of the red cabbage. If you prefer, you could serve the corn cobs whole alongside the salad rather than adding the kernels to it. For something more substantial, try tossing through some noodles, peanuts and smoked tofu cubes. It can easily be doubled up to serve more for a family gathering.

200g (7oz) red cabbage, finely shredded

200g (7oz) cherry tomatoes, halved

2 tbsp cashew butter

1 tbsp red miso paste

2 fresh corn cobs

pinch of sea salt

pinch of dried chilli flakes

1 tbsp golden syrup

1 tbsp rapeseed oil, plus extra for grilling

For the dressing

1 tbsp rapeseed oil

2 tbsp clear rice vinegar

1 tbsp tahini

1 tbsp tamari or low-sodium light soy sauce

1 large pinch of golden caster sugar

juice of 1 lemon

pinch of dried chilli flakes

Place the shredded red cabbage and cherry tomatoes in a salad bowl.

Place all the dressing ingredients in a jar, and shake well to combine. Pour this over the cabbage and tomatoes and toss to mix well. Transfer to the refrigerator while you prepare the corn.

In a small bowl, mix together the cashew butter and red miso paste. Use your hands to rub this mixture all over the corn cobs – remember to wash your hands afterwards. Season the corn with sea salt and dried chilli flakes, then drizzle over the golden syrup, followed by the rapeseed oil.

Heat a griddle pan over a medium heat and brush some rapeseed oil over the griddle. Place the corn on the griddle and cook for 1–2 minutes on each side. Turn the cobs using tongs to evenly cook on all sides. Once the kernels have turned a deep yellow and are tender but still al dente, take them off the griddle. Using a knife, carefully remove the corn kernels and add to the salad. Toss well and serve immediately.

Green Chilli, Sweetcorn, & Long-stem Broccoli on Chilled Silken Tofu

kcal — 433
carbs — 59.8g
protein — 17.6g
fat — 14.5g

Serves 4 as a side

20 min (inc. chilling time)

5 min

This is a simple, elegant and nourishing dish. I adore the contrast of the cold silken tofu with the fresh punchy hit of green chillies, ginger and spring onions in the rich, zingy sauce. This is perfect for a family buffet: the tofu can be prepared and chilled in advance, so all that is needed is a few minutes with the wok to bring everything together for the finale!

2 x 300g (10½oz) silken tofu blocks

2.5cm (1in) piece of fresh root ginger, peeled

2 green chillies, deseeded and roughly chopped

2 spring onions, trimmed and roughly chopped

1 tbsp rapeseed oil

150g (5½oz) long-stem broccoli, stalks sliced into 0.5cm (¼in) rounds and florets sliced

340g (12oz) can sweetcorn, drained

2 tbsp tamari or low-sodium light soy sauce

1 tbsp each mirin, toasted sesame oil, clear rice vinegar, lemon juice and chilli oil

sprinkling of shichimi togarashi pepper flakes, to garnish

cooked jasmine rice, to serve (see page 194)

For the drizzle

1 tbsp dark soy

1 tbsp mirin

1 tsp sesame oil

1 tbsp golden syrup or maple syrup

Carefully remove the silken tofu blocks from their packaging. Drain, and carefully place on a serving plate. Cover and chill in the refrigerator for 20 minutes.

In a small jug, whisk together all the ingredients for the drizzle and set aside.

In a small food processor, blitz the ginger, green chillies and spring onions to form a paste.

Heat a wok over a high heat and, as the wok starts to smoke, add the rapeseed oil. Once hot, add the green chilli, ginger and spring onion paste and stir for 1 second. Then add the long-stem broccoli and cook, stirring, for a few seconds. Add the sweetcorn and stir for a few seconds more, then stir in the tamari or light soy sauce, mirin, toasted sesame oil, rice vinegar, lemon juice and chilli oil. Take off the heat.

Remove the chilled silken tofu from the refrigerator and spoon the hot broccoli and sweetcorn mixture over the top. Garnish with a dusting of shichimi togarashi pepper flakes and serve immediately with some jasmine rice. Pour over the drizzle.

Waikiki Bowl

Serves 3

15 min

18–23 min

Hawaii has to be one of my favourite places in the world, with its beautiful beaches, delicious poke bowls and the nature-loving and 'aloha' spirit of 'love' of the people. This is my version of one of the nutritious, vibrant poke bowls. It's a fresh, fruity, savoury, brightly coloured bowl with sweet and more-ish salty flavours on a bed of coconut-flavoured rice.

8 cherry tomatoes, halved

1 tbsp tamari or low-sodium light soy sauce

1 tbsp finely chopped chives

200g (7oz) jasmine rice

50ml (2fl oz) coconut milk (see tip)

1 tbsp toasted coconut flakes

1 tsp rapeseed oil

2 garlic cloves, finely chopped

2.5cm (1in) piece of fresh root ginger, grated

200g (7oz) smoked tofu, drained, rinsed in cold water and diced into 1.5cm (¾in) cubes

2 tbsp mirin

2 tbsp tamari or low-sodium light soy sauce

1 tbsp golden syrup

1 kiwi, peeled and sliced into 0.5cm (¼in) rounds, then each round into 8 wedges

1 small pineapple, peeled, cored and diced into 0.5cm (¼in) cubes

1 whole mango, peeled, stoned and diced into 0.5cm (¼in) cubes

handful of roasted salted cashew nuts

handful of edamame, blanched from frozen, ready to eat

50g (1¾oz) red cabbage, shredded

fried crispy salted seaweed, 2–3 pieces of hand-torn crispy fried ready-to-eat nori, fried shallots and toasted sesame seeds, to garnish

In a small bowl, combine the cherry tomatoes with the tamari or light soy sauce and chopped chives and set aside.

Place the jasmine rice in a saucepan with the coconut milk and 350ml (12fl oz) water. Bring to the boil over a high heat. Reduce the heat to low to bring to a simmer, then cover and cook for 15–20 minutes. Once cooked, remove the lid and fluff up the rice with a fork. Sprinkle over the toasted coconut flakes and set aside.

Heat a wok over a high heat until smoking, and add the rapeseed oil. Once hot, add the garlic and ginger. Toss for a few seconds, then add the smoked tofu and cook, tossing, for 5 seconds. Add the mirin, tamari or light soy sauce and golden syrup and cook for 2–3 minutes until the sauce is reduced and the tofu is sticky. Set aside.

When you're ready to serve, divide the rice between three bowls. Working in sections (like slices of a pizza) add the various toppings to the rice: the tamari-chive tomatoes, the teriyaki tofu, the kiwi, the pineapple, the mango, the cashew nuts, the edamame and the red cabbage.

Finally, garnish with crushed crispy fried salted seaweed, nori flakes, fried shallots and toasted sesame seeds. Serve immediately.

Ching's Tip — If the coconut milk has separated in the can, stir the milk to bring it back together before using.

Thai Minced Soy & Cauliflower 'Laab'

kcal — 385
carbs — 24.7g
protein — 28.5g
fat — 19.6g

Serves 2

15 min   3–4 min

This is inspired by the Thai 'laab' salad, which traditionally uses minced pork or chicken. Here I use minced soy and cauliflower florets, whizzed up with fresh aromatics like garlic, ginger, chillies and lemongrass. It is then wok-fried and served on a bed of gem lettuce, citrus fruit and roasted peanuts, along with spring onions for a fresh bite. This is super tasty and satisfying.

100g (3½oz) dehydrated minced soy

200ml (7fl oz) hot vegetable stock or boiling water

2 garlic cloves, finely chopped

2.5cm (1in) piece of fresh root ginger, finely chopped

1 red chilli, deseeded and finely chopped

1 lemongrass stalk, finely grated using a microplane

100g (3½oz) cauliflower florets

1 tsp golden caster sugar

zest and juice of 1 lime

2 tbsp rapeseed oil

1 tbsp mirin

1 tbsp dark soy sauce

1 tbsp tamari or low-sodium light soy sauce

pinch of sea salt

pinch of ground white pepper

To serve

2 heads of little gem lettuce, leaves separated

1 lime; ½ juiced, ½ sliced into wedges

½ red chilli, deseeded and finely sliced

2 spring onions, trimmed and finely chopped

½ grapefruit or pomelo, peeled, small segments separated

small handful of roasted peanuts

To rehydrate the minced soy, add the hot water or stock and leave to stand for 5 minutes.

Place the garlic, ginger, chilli, lemongrass, soy mince, cauliflower, sugar and lime zest and juice in a food processor. Blitz to combine well. You are aiming for a granule-like texture.

Heat a wok over a high heat until smoking and add the rapeseed oil. Once hot, add the fragrant minced soy mixture and stir-fry for 1–2 minutes until slightly golden at the edges. Stir in the mirin, dark soy sauce, tamari or light soy sauce, sea salt and ground white pepper.

Arrange the lettuce leaves on two plates, then top with the minced soy mixture. Squeeze over the lime juice and garnish with lime wedges, chilli, spring onions, grapefruit or pomelo and roasted peanuts.

4.

Fast
&
Furious

Cauliflower, Chilli & Sweetcorn Chow Mein

kcal — 344
carbs — 26.9g
protein — 27.8g
fat — 12.1g

Serves 2 as a main
or 4 as a side

10 min · 3 min

This straightforward but tasty chow mein is a firm favourite with my family. The chilli bean paste gives it a bit of a kick – a little goes a long way, so adjust to your tastes. Enjoy!

100g (3½oz) soybean noodles

1 tsp toasted sesame oil

1 tbsp cornflour

1 tbsp rapeseed oil

1 red chilli, deseeded and finely chopped

200g (7oz) cauliflower florets, separated into bite-sized pieces

100g (3½oz) canned or fresh sweetcorn kernels

1 tsp dark soy sauce

1 tsp chilli bean paste

1 tsp fermented salted black beans

1 tbsp tamari or low-sodium light soy sauce

2 tbsp Shaohsing rice wine or dry sherry

100ml (3½fl oz) vegetable stock

pinch of caster sugar

1 large spring onion, trimmed and finely sliced on the angle, to garnish

Cook the soybean noodles according to the packet instructions. Drain, rinse in water and drizzle with the toasted sesame oil to prevent them from sticking. Set aside.

In a cup or small bowl, mix the cornflour with 2 tbsp water to make a slurry. Set aside until needed.

Heat a wok over a high heat. Once it's smoking, add the rapeseed oil. Once hot, add the chilli and stir for a few seconds, then add the cauliflower florets and cook, tossing, for 1 minute. Add the sweetcorn and follow with the dark soy, chilli bean paste, fermented salted black beans, tamari or light soy sauce and rice wine or sherry. Toss well and cook for 30 seconds.

Pour in the stock, add the sugar and bring to the bubble. Add the cornflour slurry and mix together well. Add the cooked noodles and stir-fry for another minute.

Serve immediately, garnished with the spring onion.

Five Spice Seitan
& Sweetheart Cabbage
with Sweetcorn & Chilli

Serves 2

10 min   5 min

Chewy seitan, sweet cabbage and crunchy sweetcorn kernels marry perfectly with Chinese five spice, chilli and soy to make a quick and satisfying dinner.

1 tbsp cornflour

1 tbsp rapeseed oil

2 garlic cloves, crushed and finely chopped

2.5cm (1in) piece of fresh root ginger, finely chopped

1 cayenne chilli, deseeded and finely chopped

200g (7oz) seitan pieces, drained and sliced into strips on the angle

pinch of Chinese five spice

1 tsp dark soy sauce

1 tbsp Shaohsing rice wine

200g (7oz) sweetheart cabbage leaves, sliced into 2.5cm (1in) strips

kernels from 1 fresh corn cob

60ml (4 tbsp) hot vegetable stock

2 tbsp tamari or low-sodium light soy sauce

dash of toasted sesame oil

1 large spring onion, trimmed and finely sliced on the angle, to garnish

In a cup or small bowl, mix the cornflour with 2 tbsp water to make a slurry. Set aside until needed.

Heat a wok over a high heat until smoking, and add the rapeseed oil. Give the oil a swirl around the wok, then add the garlic, ginger and chilli. Stir-fry for a few seconds, then add the seitan pieces. Stir in the Chinese five spice, dark soy and rice wine and cook for a few seconds, tossing all the while.

Add the sweetheart cabbage leaves and the corn kernels and cook for 2–3 minutes, then stir in the vegetable stock and tamari or light soy. Once the vegetables are softened but still al dente, add the cornflour slurry and toss together well to coat the vegetables.

Season with a dash of toasted sesame oil and sprinkle over the spring onion, then serve immediately.

Sweet & Sour 2.0 – Jackfruit, Seitan, Pineapple, Peppers & Chickpeas

kcal — 570
carbs — 115.4g
protein — 16.0g
fat — 7.8g

Serves 4

15 min   5 min

I love a classic sweet and sour sauce. This is my staple recipe and it's very versatile. You can add whatever ingredients you like – try sweetcorn, mushrooms, courgettes or tofu – but here I have opted for the sweet and fruity meatiness of jackfruit, seitan, fresh pineapple, crunchy peppers and water chestnuts. This is one of my go-to mid-week suppers and is excellent with jasmine rice.

1 tbsp rapeseed oil

2.5cm (1in) piece of fresh root ginger, grated

1 red chilli, deseeded and finely chopped

400g (14oz) can jackfruit pieces, drained and chopped into 2.5cm (1in) chunks

100g (3½oz) seitan pieces, drained, sliced into 2.5cm (1in) chunks

1 tbsp Shaohsing rice wine or dry sherry

1 red pepper, deseeded and chopped into 1.5cm (¾in) pieces

½ small pineapple, peeled, cored and diced into 1.5cm (¾in) cubes

225g (8oz) can water chestnuts, drained, whole or sliced

½ 400g (14oz) can chickpeas, drained and rinsed

small handful of roasted salted cashew nuts

1 spring onion, trimmed and finely sliced

cooked jasmine rice, to serve (see page 194)

For the sweet & sour sauce

150ml (5fl oz) pineapple juice

1 tbsp tamari or low-sodium light soy sauce

1 tbsp cornflour

juice of 1 lime

1 tsp golden syrup

½ tsp sriracha

In a small jug, whisk together all the sauce ingredients and set aside.

Heat a wok over a high heat. When the wok starts to smoke, add the rapeseed oil. Once hot, add the ginger and chilli, frying for a few seconds to release their flavour. Add the jackfruit pieces and cook, tossing, for a few seconds. Add the seitan and stir-fry for a few seconds, then add the Shaohsing rice wine or sherry, pepper, pineapple, water chestnuts and chickpeas and toss together for 1 minute, until the peppers are slightly soft but still crisp.

Pour over the sauce and bring to the bubble. Add the cashew nuts and toss well to coat all the ingredients in the sauce.

Scatter over the spring onions and serve immediately with jasmine rice.

Spicy Sichuan King Trumpet Mushrooms

kcal — 410
carbs — 80.3g
protein — 10.0g
fat — 7.6g

Serves 2

5 min

10 min

This is my vegan version of a famous Sichuan pork dish, *Hui guo rou*, where the meat is boiled in an aromatic stock, then sliced and fried until crisp, and finally stir-fried with chilli, fermented salted black beans and a host of Chinese seasonings. Instead of pork, I am using meaty king trumpet mushrooms. This dish is perfect served with jasmine rice.

1 tbsp rapeseed oil

1 tbsp freshly grated root ginger

300g (10½oz) king trumpet mushrooms, sliced into 1cm (½in) rounds

1 tbsp Shaohsing rice wine or dry sherry

1 tbsp chilli bean paste

1 tbsp yellow bean paste

1 tbsp fermented salted black beans, rinsed and crushed

1 spring onion, trimmed and sliced on the angle into julienne strips (optional)

1 tsp dark soy sauce

1 tsp tamari or low-sodium light soy sauce

pinch of golden granulated or caster sugar

pinch of ground white pepper

cooked jasmine rice, to serve (see page 194)

Place a wok over a high heat until smoking, then add the rapeseed oil. Once hot, add the ginger and cook, tossing, for few seconds, then add the mushrooms. As they start to brown, add the rice wine or sherry, then stir in the chilli bean paste and the yellow bean paste, followed by the fermented salted black beans. Add the spring onions, if using, and stir-fry for less than a minute.

Season with the dark soy sauce, tamari or light soy sauce, sugar and ground white pepper and give it all one final toss. Serve immediately with jasmine rice.

Wok-Fried Sichuan Orange King Trumpet Mushrooms

kcal — 491
carbs — 91.6g
protein — 14.9g
fat — 9.0g

Serves 2

15 min

3 min

Traditionally this dish uses beef, but I love the meatiness of king trumpet mushrooms – they make this dish so more-ish. If you can't find them, you can use shiitake mushrooms instead, or any mushrooms of your choice. This is such a delicious and quick mid-week supper and is perfect with jasmine rice or noodles.

4 large king trumpet mushrooms, tops sliced, and stalks sliced into long, thin, rectangular slices about 1 x 2cm (½ x¾in) in size

1 tbsp rapeseed oil

2 garlic cloves, finely chopped

3 bulbs of baby pak choi, halved

100g (3½oz) mangetout

1 tbsp Shaohsing rice wine or dry sherry

1 tbsp tamari or low-sodium light soy sauce

large pinch of ground white pepper

1 tsp toasted sesame oil

cooked jasmine rice, to serve (see page 194)

For the marinade

1 tsp shop-bought chilli-garlic sauce

½ tsp ground Sichuan pepper

2 tbsp tamari

1 tbsp golden syrup

4 tbsp freshly squeezed orange juice

1 tsp dark soy sauce

Prepare the marinade. In a bowl, combine all the marinade ingredients and stir well to combine. Add the mushroom slices and leave to marinate for 5 minutes.

Heat a wok over a high heat until smoking, and add the rapeseed oil. Once hot, add the garlic and stir-fry for a few seconds. Now add the marinated mushroom slices (reserving any liquid) and stir-fry for 10 seconds. Add the baby pack choi halves and stir-fry for a further 30 seconds, followed by the mangetout. Stir-fry for 30 seconds more.

Stir in the rice wine or sherry along with the tamari or soy sauce and any remaining marinade liquid. Cook, tossing all the while, for about 20 seconds to reduce the sauce.

Add the ground white pepper and sesame oil, give it all one final toss, and serve immediately with jasmine rice.

Smoked Tofu Zhajiang Noodles

Serves 4

15 min 9 min

Zhajiang mein means 'mixed sauce noodle'. Traditional *Zhajiang* noodles are made with fresh, hand-pulled noodles. It is a classic Beijing dish. There are many different variations, and some are saucier than others, but I like the traditional version, which is slightly drier. I like to add minced garlic as well as the traditional leeks and ginger for the aromatics. I have used smoked tofu here; the trick is to fry it in the wok until it is slightly crisp.

200g (7oz) wheat-flour noodles

2 tbsp rapeseed oil

3 garlic cloves, finely chopped

2.5cm (1in) piece fresh root ginger, finely grated

2 baby leeks, diced

1 tsp Sichuan peppercorns

200g (7oz) smoked tofu, drained, rinsed in cold water and finely chopped into 0.5cm (¼in) cubes

1 tbsp of Shaohsing rice wine

1 tsp fragrant oil (such as the Ginger & Spring Onion Infused Oil on page 197)

1 tbsp dark soy sauce

200ml (7fl oz) vegetable stock

2 tsp tian mian jiang or hoisin sauce

1 tsp yellow bean paste or miso

To serve

1 tbsp sesame oil

1 tsp tamari or low-sodium light soy sauce

1 tsp chilli sauce

drizzle of chilli oil

2 small radishes, sliced into matchsticks

½ cucumber, deseeded and sliced into matchsticks

1 spring onion, trimmed and finely chopped

Cook the noodles according to the packet instructions, then drain.

Take four serving bowls and, into each one, pour half the sesame oil, tamari or light soy sauce, chilli sauce and a dash of chilli oil. Place the cooked noodles on top and set aside.

Heat a wok over a high heat until smoking, then add the rapeseed oil. Once hot, add the garlic, ginger, leeks and Sichuan peppercorns and toss in the heat for a few seconds. Then add the smoked tofu, and stir-fry together for a minute.

Add the rice wine, fragrant oil and dark soy sauce and stir-fry together for another minute. Next, add the stock, along with the tian mian jiang or hoisin sauce and yellow bean paste. Toss together well. Cook for 2 minutes, stirring, until the tofu is slightly crisp.

Divide the tofu between the four bowls and garnish with the cucumber and radish matchsticks and the spring onion. Serve immediately. Toss and mix all the ingredients together well before eating.

Five Spice Mixed Mushroom Soba Chow Mein

kcal — 471
carbs — 73.0g
protein — 19.5g
fat — 10.6g

Serves 2 or 4 as a side

15 min 5 min

This is a delicious, easy chow mein (which means 'stirred noodle'). The five spice, ginger and mushrooms work so well together. The delicate buckwheat noodles just need warming through and a gentle toss at the end. The trick is to not overcook them (just follow the packet instructions), and then rinse them well in cold water before you add them to the wok so they keep their 'bite'.

200g (7oz) buckwheat noodles

toasted sesame oil, for drizzling

1 tbsp rapeseed oil

2 garlic cloves, finely chopped

1 tbsp freshly grated root ginger

1 red chilli, deseeded and finely chopped

300g (10½oz) white shimeji mushrooms, separated

1 tsp Chinese five spice

1 tsp dark soy sauce

1 tbsp Shaohsing rice wine

1 red pepper, deseeded and cut into julienne strips

2 large handfuls of beansprouts, washed

1 tbsp tamari or low-sodium light soy sauce

2 spring onions, trimmed and cut into julienne strips, to garnish

Prepare the buckwheat noodles according to the packet instructions, then rinse well in cold water. Drizzle over some toasted sesame oil and set aside until needed.

Place a wok over a high heat until smoking, then add the rapeseed oil. Once hot, add the garlic, ginger and chilli and stir for a few seconds. Next add the mushrooms and the Chinese five spice. Season with the dark soy and Shaohsing rice wine and cook, tossing, for a few seconds.

Add the buckwheat noodles, along with the red pepper and beansprouts and toss well. Stir in the tamari or light soy sauce, garnish with the spring onions and serve immediately.

Black Bean, Mushroom, Seitan & Green Pepper Stir-Fry

kcal — 519
carbs — 88.6g
protein — 26.5g
fat — 7.9g

Serves 2

10 min   5 min

This is a delicious, more-ish stir-fry. The mushrooms give a juicy sweetness and the seitan adds texture, while the green peppers offer a crunchy bite. A speedy supper that's perfect with jasmine rice.

1 tsp cornflour

1 tbsp rapeseed oil

2 shallots, peeled and sliced

1 red chilli, deseeded and finely chopped

150g (5½oz) seitan pieces, drained, and sliced on the angle into 0.5cm (¼in) slices

100g (3½oz) white button mushrooms, quartered

1 green pepper, diced into 1cm (½in) cubes

1 tsp shop-bought black bean sauce

1 tbsp Shaohsing rice wine or dry sherry

1 tbsp tamari or low-sodium light soy sauce

1 tsp shop-bought vegetarian mushroom sauce

½ tsp dark soy sauce

pinch of golden caster sugar

cooked jasmine rice, to serve (see page 194)

In a cup or small bowl, mix the cornflour with 2 tbsp water to make a slurry. Set aside until needed.

Heat a wok over a high heat until smoking, then add the rapeseed oil. Once hot, add the shallots and stir-fry for a few seconds, then add the chilli, seitan slices, mushrooms and green pepper. Stir in the black bean sauce and cook, tossing, for 1 minute until the vegetables are seared and slightly browned at the edges. Stir in the rice wine or dry sherry.

Add the tamari or light soy sauce, along with the mushroom sauce, dark soy sauce and sugar. Bring any juices in the wok to the bubble, then stir through the cornflour slurry to thicken the sauce until it coats the vegetables. Spoon on to plates and serve with jasmine rice.

Three-cup Tofu & Baby Courgettes

kcal — 372
carbs — 46.9g
protein — 13.0g
fat — 15.1g

Serves 4 as a side

5 min   7 min

This dish has one of my all-time favourite flavour profiles. It's usually wokked up using chicken, but I use ready-to-cook fried tofu instead, as the dish becomes even more delightful when you bite into a piece of tofu and the sauce oozes out. Baby courgettes soak up the sauce brilliantly, too, and provide a soft yet slightly al dente texture.

1 tbsp rapeseed oil

2.5cm (1in) piece of fresh root ginger, sliced into rounds

2 garlic cloves, crushed and peeled, but left whole

1 red chilli, sliced

250g (9oz) ready-fried tofu, each piece quartered into triangular pieces, washed and patted dry (or regular tofu, frozen overnight and defrosted – see recipe introduction on page 86)

100g (3½oz) baby courgettes, sliced on the diagonal into 1cm (½in) ovals

1 tbsp Shaohsing rice wine or dry sherry

50ml (2fl oz) tamari or low-sodium light soy sauce

1 tbsp toasted sesame oil

1 tsp caster sugar

1 small handful Thai basil leaves

cooked jasmine rice, to serve (see page 194)

Heat a wok over a high heat until smoking, then add the rapeseed oil. Once hot, add the ginger slices and fry until golden and crispy, then add the garlic and chilli and toss for a few seconds to release their flavours.

Add the fried tofu pieces. Leave for 5 seconds to sear, then flip them over. Add the baby courgette slices and pour over the rice wine or dry sherry. Stir-fry for 1 minute to sear the baby courgettes.

Add the tamari or light soy sauce, toasted sesame oil and sugar and cook for 2 minutes until the liquid has evaporated. The sauce should be dark, with a slightly sticky shine, and the courgettes should be softened but still a little al dente. Add the Thai basil leaves and toss through to wilt, then take off the heat and serve with jasmine rice.

Minced Soy & French Bean Stir-fry

kcal — 286
carbs — 43.6g
protein — 15.3g
fat — 6.9g

Serves 4 as a side

10 min   5 min

This is a stir-fry inspired by a lunch I had with my *Ah-e* (aunty) in Beijing. She cooked a simple but tasty chicken and snake bean stir-fry, and this is my quick, vegan version. Serve with jasmine rice. To turn this into a noodle dish, just add your favourite noodles at the end, toss through and adjust seasoning further to taste if needed.

100g (3½oz) dehydrated minced soy

200ml (7fl oz) hot vegetable stock or boiling water

1 tbsp rapeseed oil

1 garlic clove, crushed

1 tbsp Shaohsing rice wine

2 tbsp dark soy sauce

100g (3½oz) French beans, trimmed, lightly crushed using the side of a large knife or Chinese cleaver, then sliced on the angle into 1cm (½in) pieces

1 tbsp cashew nuts, toasted

1 tbsp tamari or low-sodium light soy sauce

dash of toasted sesame oil

pinch of ground white pepper

small handful of coriander leaves, to garnish

cooked jasmine rice, to serve (see page 194)

To rehydrate the minced soy, add the hot water or stock and leave to stand for 5 minutes.

Place a wok over a high heat until smoking, then add 1 tbsp rapeseed oil. Once hot, add the garlic and stir for a second. Add the rehydrated minced soy and cook, tossing, for a few seconds. Add the rice wine and dark soy sauce and cook, stirring, for 30 seconds.

Push the soy mince to one side of the wok. Add the remaining 1 tbsp rapeseed oil to the other side of the wok. Once hot, add the French beans. Cook them, tossing, for 2–3 minutes, until softened but still al dente.

Add the cashews, and season with tamari or light soy sauce, sesame oil and ground white pepper. Stir everything together and garnish with the coriander leaves. Serve immediately with jasmine rice.

Black Bean Tofu & Baby Pak Choi

kcal — 397
carbs — 53.4g
protein — 15.4g
fat — 14.0g

Serves 4 as a side

15 min   8 min

I add a touch of a good-quality yellow bean sauce to give this dish a savoury, mellow edge. If you are able to buy ready-fried tofu from a Chinese supermarket, it has a sponge-like quality which is super delicious and a quick cheat. Alternatively, place a block of tofu in the freezer overnight, then defrost before use. The water crystals will produce large 'pores' in the tofu that make it extra 'spongy', helping it absorb lots of sauce, and therefore, flavour!

1 tbsp cornflour

1 tbsp rapeseed oil

5 garlic cloves, finely chopped

1 tbsp freshly grated root ginger

1 red chilli, deseeded and chopped

1 bird's eye chilli, deseeded and chopped

1 tbsp fermented salted black beans, rinsed and crushed

1 tbsp yellow bean paste or miso paste

250g (9oz) ready-fried tofu (or regular tofu – see page 12), quartered

1 tbsp Shaohsing rice wine or dry sherry

2 green peppers, deseeded and cut into 1.5cm (¾in) chunks

200ml (7fl oz) vegetable stock

1 tbsp tamari or low-sodium light soy sauce

cooked jasmine rice, to serve (see page 194)

For the pak choi

200g (7oz) baby pak choi, halved

pinch of sea salt

1 tbsp Shaohsing rice wine

1 tbsp tamari or low-sodium light soy sauce

1 tsp toasted sesame oil

2.5cm (1in) piece of fresh root ginger, sliced into matchsticks

First, prepare the pak choi. Place a heatproof plate inside a bamboo steamer. Season the pak choi with salt, rice wine, tamari or light soy sauce and toasted sesame oil, then lay the ginger slices over the top. Place the lid on the steamer and set over a wok or pan of water. Bring to the boil, then gently steam over a low heat for 3–4 minutes.

In a small jug or cup, mix the cornflour with 2 tbsp water to create a slurry and set aside until needed.

Meanwhile, place a wok over a high heat and add the rapeseed oil. When the oil starts to smoke, add the garlic, ginger and chillies and stir-fry for a few seconds. Then add the black beans and yellow bean paste and stir quickly.

Add the tofu and stir-fry for 1 minute, keeping the ingredients moving in the wok, then add the rice wine or sherry and the green peppers and stir-fry for a further minute.

Add the stock and bring to the boil. Season with the tamari or soy sauce, then add the cornflour slurry and stir to thicken.

Serve the black bean tofu and steamed baby pak choi with jasmine rice on the side and eat immediately.

Buddha's Mixed Vegetable Stir-fry

kcal — 334
carbs — 52.3g
protein — 9.3g
fat — 10.6g

Serves 4 as a side

15 min   3–4 min

This is the kind of stir-fry I make when I have leftovers in my refrigerator that need using up. You can add whatever you like, but I think simple meals like this are sometimes best served with just jasmine rice and perhaps a tablespoon of the Ginger & Spring Onion Infused Oil on page 197. If you need some protein, add slices of smoked tofu after the pak choi. Instead of jasmine rice, you could add some cooked noodles of your choice after the pak choi to turn it into a veggie chow mein.

1 tbsp rapeseed oil

2.5cm (1in) piece of fresh root ginger, grated

1 large carrot, sliced into julienne strips

1 tbsp Shaohsing rice wine or dry sherry

10 fresh shiitake mushrooms, sliced

225g (8oz) can water chestnuts, drained and sliced into thin rounds

225g (8oz) can bamboo shoots, drained and sliced into julienne strips

200g (7oz) baby corn, sliced in half down the middle

2 baby pak choi, leaves separated

100g (3½oz) beansprouts, washed

2 large spring onions, trimmed and sliced into julienne strips

1 large handful toasted cashew nuts

cooked jasmine rice, to serve (see page 194)

For the sauce

100ml (3½fl oz) cold vegetable stock

1–2 tbsp tamari or low-sodium light soy sauce

1 tbsp each vegetarian mushroom sauce, toasted sesame oil, rice vinegar and cornflour

Place all the ingredients for the sauce in a jug. Mix well to combine and set aside.

Heat a wok over a high heat until smoking, then add the rapeseed oil. Once hot, add the ginger and stir-fry for a few seconds. Now add the carrot and stir-fry for 1 minute, then season with the rice wine or sherry.

Add the shiitake mushrooms, water chestnuts, bamboo shoots, baby corn and pak choi leaves. Cook, stirring together, for 1 minute.

Pour in the sauce and bring to the bubble. Now add the beansprouts and spring onions and give it one last stir together.

Sprinkle over the toasted cashew nuts and serve immediately with jasmine rice.

Kung Po Lotus Root

Serves 2

5 min

8–9 min

This is a great Sichuan dish that was invented by Ding Baochen, a governor of Sichuan. *Gong Bao,* also known as *Kung Po*, means 'palatial guardian'. The dish is still named in honour of him. I adore the spicy, sweet and tangy flavours of this dish, and the crunchy, nutty addition of the lotus root. Do seek it out at the Chinese supermarket if you can. Otherwise, you can use canned water chestnuts or ready-fried tofu – both make equally delicious substitutes. Perfect served with jasmine rice.

200g (7oz) lotus root, about 4cm (1½in) in diameter, peeled and sliced into 0.5cm (¼in) rounds (or semicircles if the roots are too large)

1 tbsp rapeseed oil

1 tbsp Sichuan peppercorns

3 whole dried chillies

1 tbsp Shaohsing rice wine

1 small red pepper, chopped into 2cm (¾in) chunks

handful of dry-roasted peanuts or cashew nuts

2 spring onions, trimmed and sliced on the angle

cooked jasmine rice, to serve (see page 194)

For the sauce

100ml (3½fl oz) cold vegetable stock

1 tbsp tamari or low-sodium light soy sauce

1 tbsp tomato ketchup

1 tbsp Chinkiang black rice vinegar

1 tsp sriracha or good chilli sauce

1 tbsp cornflour

Blanch the sliced lotus root in boiled hot water for 1–2 minutes, then drain and set aside.

Place all the sauce ingredients in a small jug and mix well to combine, then set aside.

Heat a wok over a high heat until smoking, then add the rapeseed oil. Once hot, add the Sichuan peppercorns and dried chillies and fry for a few seconds. Then add the blanched lotus and stir-fry for 1 minute or until the lotus root slices are seared at the edges. Add the rice wine and red pepper and cook, stirring, for less than 30 seconds.

Pour in the sauce ingredients and bring to the boil. When the sauce has reduced to a thicker, slightly sticky consistency, add the dry-roasted nuts, followed by the spring onions, and cook for 1 minute, stirring together well.

Transfer to a serving plate and serve immediately with jasmine rice.

Yuxiang Aubergine
with Shiitake Mushrooms

kcal — 505
carbs — 87.8g
protein — 10.0g
fat — 14.9g

Serves 2 as a main
or 4 as a side

10 min   10 min

This warming, comforting meal hails from the Sichuan province
in China. It's a go-to staple for a mid-week supper. Aubergines are rich
in vitamin E and shiitake mushrooms are full of antioxidants. To mix it up,
I sometimes switch the shiitake for smoked tofu – both are equally good.

2 tbsp rapeseed oil

200g (7oz) baby aubergines, trimmed and sliced into
quarters lengthways

2 garlic cloves, finely chopped

2.5cm (1in) piece of fresh root ginger, finely grated

1 red chilli, deseeded and finely chopped

1 tbsp chilli bean paste

200g (7oz) fresh shiitake mushrooms, sliced

2 spring onions, trimmed and finely sliced

small handful of coriander, stalks finely chopped,
leaves separated

cooked jasmine rice, to serve (see page 194)

For the sauce

100ml (3½fl oz) cold vegetable stock

1 tbsp tamari or low-sodium light soy sauce

1 tbsp Chinese black rice vinegar

1 tsp toasted sesame oil

pinch of caster sugar

1 tbsp cornflour

Place all the ingredients for the sauce in a jug.
Stir well and set aside until needed.

Heat a wok over a high heat until smoking, then
add 1 tbsp rapeseed oil. Once hot, add the aubergine
and cook, stirring, for 5 minutes, until browned.
As you cook it, keep adding drops of water, up to
about 50ml (2fl oz) in total. This will create steam to
help soften the aubergine (much healthier than frying
it in lots of oil). Once cooked, transfer the aubergine
to a plate and set aside.

Return the empty wok to the heat and add the
remaining 1 tbsp rapeseed oil. Add the garlic, ginger,
chilli and chilli bean paste and stir for a few seconds.
Return the cooked aubergine to the wok and add the
sliced shiitake mushrooms. Pour over the sauce and
bring to the bubble, cooking for 3–4 minutes on high
heat until the sauce thickens.

Stir in the spring onions and coriander stalks. Garnish
with the coriander leaves and serve immediately with
jasmine rice.

Sweetcorn Dan Dan Noodles

kcal — 375
carbs — 37.2g
protein — 23.1g
fat — 15.0g

Serves 6

15 min   15 min

Dan Dan Noodles are a Sichuan pepper-spiced street food classic, and here I've given them a little update with the use of sweetcorn to add sweetness and texture. You can use canned sweetcorn or fresh corn kernels, or swap them out completely for diced French beans or edamame. Mix it up and use what you have – it's versatile and delicious.

250g (9oz) wide wheat-flour noodles (flat Japanese udon)

1 tsp toasted sesame oil

2 tbsp rapeseed oil

2 garlic cloves, finely chopped

2.5cm (1in) piece of fresh root ginger, grated

3 red chillies, deseeded and finely chopped

200g (7oz) dehydrated minced soy

1 tbsp Shaoshing rice wine or dry sherry

2 tbsp dark soy sauce

1 tbsp Chinkiang black rice vinegar

1 tbsp tamari or low-sodium light soy sauce

1 tbsp tahini

1 tsp ground Sichuan peppercorns

340g (12oz) can sweetcorn, drained

freshly ground white pepper, to taste

For the chilli topping

6 tsp each chilli oil, toasted sesame oil and tamari or low-sodium light soy sauce

6 small pinches of ground Sichuan peppercorns

3 tbsp finely diced, deseeded red chilli

To serve

800ml (1½ pints) very hot vegetable stock

3 tbsp finely chopped spring onions

small handful of fresh coriander, finely chopped

To make the noodles, bring a large pot of water to the boil over a high heat. Add the noodles and stir. Cook for about 4 minutes until al dente. Drain, rinse with cold water, shake out any excess water and transfer them to a bowl. Pour the sesame oil over the noodles and toss well to coat. Set aside until needed.

Heat a wok over a high heat until smoking, and add the rapeseed oil. Once hot, add the garlic, ginger and chillies and stir-fry for 30 seconds. Add the minced soy and cook, breaking up with a spatula, for 2–3 minutes until browned. Add the rice wine or sherry, dark soy sauce, black rice vinegar, tamari or light soy sauce, tahini and ground peppercorns, and stir well until the minced soy begins to crisp a little. Add the sweetcorn and toss to mix well, cooking for another minute. Season the mix with ground white pepper and remove from the heat.

To prepare the chilli topping, mix together the chilli oil, sesame oil, tamari or light soy sauce, ground peppercorns and chillies in a small bowl.

To serve, divide the noodles between six deep soup bowls and sprinkle the minced soy topping evenly over each bowl. Pour the hot stock evenly over the noodles, then drizzle over the chilli topping evenly over each bowl. Scatter over the spring onions and coriander and serve immediately.

General Tso's Cauliflower & Sweetcorn

Serves 2

15 min   8 min

There are many variations of this recipe all over the world. It was invented by a Hunanese man named Peng-Chang Kuei. He was a Chinese Nationalist Party chef and cooked for state banquets and official events. When he first came up with the dish in the 1950s, its original flavours were Hunanese: hot, sour, salty and heavy. However, when he moved to New York in 1973, he had to adapt the dish to make it sweeter to suit American palates – and General Tso's was born. The original dish used chicken, but here I've used cauliflower florets.

1 small head of cauliflower, cut into bite-sized florets

1 tbsp rapeseed oil

1 garlic clove, peeled and crushed, but left whole

4 whole dried Sichuan chillies

1 onion, chopped into 2.5cm (1in) pieces

340g (12oz) can sweetcorn

1 large red pepper, chopped into 2.5cm (1in) pieces

1 tbsp Shaohsing rice wine or dry sherry

4 spring onions, trimmed and chopped into 2.5cm (1in) pieces

1 small handful of peanuts, toasted and chopped, optional

toasted sesame seeds, to garnish

cooked jasmine rice, to serve (see page 194)

For the sauce

1 tbsp yellow bean sauce

2 tbsp tamari or low-sodium light soy sauce

1 tbsp tomato purée

1 tbsp rice vinegar

1 tbsp chilli sauce

1 tsp light brown sugar

1 tsp dark soy sauce

Blanch the cauliflower florets in 500ml (18fl oz) boiling water for 30 seconds, then drain and set aside.

Place all the sauce ingredients in a small bowl or jug. Mix together and set aside.

Heat a wok over a high heat. When the wok starts to smoke, add the rapeseed oil, followed by the garlic and chillies. Fry for a few seconds, then add the onion and stir-fry for 1 minute.

Add the blanched cauliflower florets and stir-fry for 2 minutes until softened. Stir in the sweetcorn, red pepper and rice wine or sherry. Pour in the sauce and cook until the sauce has reduced to a thicker, slightly sticky consistency. Add the spring onions and peanuts, if using, and toss to combine.

Transfer to a serving plate and garnish with the sesame seeds. Serve with jasmine rice.

Ching's Tip — This dish is very versatile, so you can experiment. Instead of cauliflower, you can use whatever you prefer: broccoli, smoked firm tofu, ready-fried tofu, meaty shiitake mushroom or seitan pieces.

Sticky Hoisin Broccoli with Toasted Almonds

kcal — 442
carbs — 77.5g
protein — 18.1g
fat — 6.8g

Serves 2

10 min

7 min

Sweet broccoli is tossed in a spicy orange and hoisin sauce, while toasted flaked almonds add a nutty bite. The trick is to char the broccoli in the wok to create smoky notes, as though it's been cooked on the barbecue. A satisfying dish perfect with added noodles (or rice), it also makes a great accompaniment to other sharing dishes.

150g (5½oz) wheat noodles (optional), to serve

1 tsp rapeseed oil

1 head of broccoli, broken into florets

handful of toasted almond flakes, to garnish

For the sauce

1 tsp freshly grated root ginger

1 red chilli, deseeded and finely chopped

1 tsp golden syrup

zest and juice of ½ small orange

1 tbsp hoisin sauce

1 tbsp tamari or low-sodium light soy sauce

1 tsp toasted sesame oil

100ml (3½fl oz) cold vegetable stock

1 tbsp cornflour

If you are adding wheat noodles, cook according to the packet instructions, and set aside.

Place all the sauce ingredients in a small jug and mix together to combine. Set aside.

Heat a wok over a high heat until smoking, then add the rapeseed oil. Once hot, add the broccoli florets and cook, stirring, for 1 minute, charring the edges slightly. Then add about 2 tbsp water around the edges of the wok. This will create some steam to help cook the florets. Cook for another minute to bring the broccoli to an al dente texture.

Now pour in the sauce and stir, coating the broccoli florets well but taking care not to break them up. Bring the sauce to the boil and cook until glossy. If you are adding noodles, add them now and toss to warm through.

Finally, garnish with toasted almond flakes and serve immediately.

Quick & Spicy Smoked Tofu & Chickpea Noodles

kcal — 591
carbs — 69.8g
protein — 31.6g
fat — 20.5g

Serves 2

15 min

5 min

When you ask for a vegetarian noodle dish in China, they often add chickpeas. I love the simplicity of this dish – it is wholesome and filling. You can add any greens or veggies you like; in fact, this recipe is ideal if you are in need of a refrigerator clear-out, as it's so versatile.

150g (5½oz) ramen noodles

toasted sesame oil, for dressing the noodles

1 tbsp rapeseed oil

200g (7oz) smoked tofu, drained, rinsed in cold water and sliced into 1.5cm (¾in) cubes

200g (7oz) chickpeas from a can, drained and rinsed

1 tbsp Shaohsing rice wine or dry sherry

1 tbsp tamari or low-sodium light soy sauce

1 tbsp dark soy sauce

100g (3½oz) Chinese leaf, sliced into 2.5cm (1in) pieces

1 tsp Chiu Chow chilli oil, to garnish

For the paste

2 garlic cloves, finely chopped

2.5cm (1in) piece of fresh root ginger, grated

1 red chilli, deseeded and finely chopped

1 spring onion, trimmed and chopped

Place the garlic, ginger, chilli and spring onion into a food processor and blitz into a paste. Set aside until needed.

Cook the noodles according to the packet instructions. Drain, refresh under cold water and drizzle with toasted sesame oil. Set aside.

Heat a wok over a high heat until smoking, then add the rapeseed oil. Once hot, add the paste and fry for a few seconds until fragrant. Now add the smoked tofu, chickpeas and rice wine or sherry, and cook, tossing, for a few seconds. Stir in the tamari or light soy sauce and dark soy sauce, followed by 700ml (1¼ pints) boiling water.

Add the Chinese leaf and bring to a simmer. Once simmering, add the cooked ramen noodles and bring to the boil once again.

Transfer to bowls and drizzle over the chilli oil. Serve immediately.

Malaysia-style Hakka Mee

kcal — 421
carbs — 70.1g
protein — 20.7g
fat — 7.7g

Serves 4

15 min   5 min

This is a gorgeous noodle dish inspired by Mee Hakka in Ipoh, Malaysia, where we had the best Hakka noodles I had ever tasted when my husband and I visited his father's hometown in 2009. I have used more vegetables, like carrot, courgettes and diced Chinese mushrooms. The noodles we had were flat egg noodles, but here I have used wide, flat rice noodles.

100g (3½oz) dehydrated minced soy

200ml (7fl oz) boiling water or hot vegetable stock

100g (3½oz) dried sliced shiitake mushrooms

1 × 200g (7oz) pack of dried flat rice 'Pad Thai'-style noodles

1 tbsp toasted sesame oil

1 tbsp rapeseed oil

1 large carrot, finely diced

1 courgette, finely diced

1 tbsp Shaohsing rice wine or dry sherry

2 tbsp dark soy sauce

2 tbsp tamari or low-sodium light soy sauce

1 tbsp vegetarian mushroom sauce

1 tsp sriracha sauce

10g (½oz) chives, finely sliced, to garnish

For the paste

2 garlic cloves

2.5cm (1in) piece of fresh root ginger, roughly chopped

2 red chillies, deseeded and roughly chopped

5 baby shallots, roughly chopped

To serve

1 red chilli, finely sliced and dressed in 1 tbsp Chinkiang black rice vinegar in a small bowl

1 garlic clove, finely minced, mixed with a dollop of spicy chilli sauce in a small bowl

To rehydrate the minced soy, add the hot water or stock and leave to stand for 5 minutes.

Soak the shiitake mushrooms in hot water for 20 minutes, then drain and finely dice.

Cook the noodles according to the packet instructions, then drain and dress with toasted sesame oil. Divide between two bowls and set aside.

To make the paste, place the garlic, ginger, chilli and baby shallots in a food processor. Blitz into a fine paste.

Heat a wok over a high heat until smoking, then add the rapeseed oil. Once hot, add the paste and cook for a few seconds until it releases its aroma.

Add the minced soy, mushrooms, carrot and courgette and cook for 1 minute.

Add the rice wine or sherry, dark soy sauce, tamari or light soy sauce, mushroom sauce and sriracha and toss well to combine the flavours.

Spoon the mushroom and minced soy mixture over the noodles. Garnish with finely chopped chives and serve with red chilli in vinegar and garlic in chilli sauce on the side. Eat immediately.

Chunky Mushroom & Tofu Laksa

kcal — 589
carbs — 24.8g
protein — 40.0g
fat — 34.7g

Serves 4

15 min

20 min

Laksa is a Malaysian-Chinese curry noodle broth and one of Malaysia's national dishes. The oyster mushrooms add a meatiness, while the sponge-like quality of the ready-fried tofu absorbs the flavours of the broth. If you can't get ready-fried tofu, freeze a block of tofu overnight, then defrost before use. It will have a similar absorbent effect.

250g (9oz) soybean noodles

1 tbsp toasted sesame oil

1 tbsp rapeseed oil

400ml (14fl oz) coconut milk

500ml (18fl oz) vegetable stock

juice of 1 lime

1 tsp soft brown sugar

1 tsp dark soy sauce

1 tbsp tamari or low-sodium light soy sauce

100g (3½oz) French beans, cut into 1cm (½in) pieces

1 large courgette, cut into 1cm (½in) half-moon slices

1 corn cob, sliced into 4 rounds

100g (3½oz) ready-fried tofu, cut into 1cm (½in) cubes

200g (7oz) oyster mushrooms, sliced

sea salt, to taste

80g (2¾oz) beansprouts

pinch of ground chilli flakes

small handful of coriander leaves

For the laksa paste

1 tsp each ground coriander, ground cumin and ground turmeric

½ onion, chopped

40ml (1½fl oz) coconut milk (see tip on page 67)

1 tbsp freshly grated root ginger or galangal

2 garlic cloves, crushed

1 lemongrass stalk, roughly chopped

1 red cayenne chilli, deseeded and roughly chopped

1 tsp tamarind paste

1 tbsp yellow bean paste or miso

Cook the soybean noodles according to the packet instructions. Drain and dress with the toasted sesame oil, then set aside.

Put all the ingredients for the laksa paste into a food processor and blend to form a smooth paste.

Heat a wok over a high heat until smoking, then add the rapeseed oil. Once it's hot, add the paste and cook for a few seconds to release its aroma. Stir in the coconut milk, stock, lime juice, sugar, dark soy sauce and tamari or light soy sauce and simmer for 15 minutes.

Add the French beans, courgette, corn, fried tofu and mushrooms and cook for 5 minutes. Season with sea salt to taste.

Divide the noodles between four bowls, then spoon over the laksa broth with the vegetables. Garnish with the crunchy beansprouts, ground chilli flakes and coriander leaves. Serve immediately.

Thai Green Seitan 'Pad Thai'

kcal — 310
carbs — 48.2g
protein — 20.7g
fat — 3.8g

Serves 4

15 min

5–6 min

Pad Thai is to Thai people what chow mein is to the Chinese. In this recipe, I have used Thai green curry paste as a stir-fry sauce to reinvent the pad thai, along with meaty seitan and assorted crispy veggies. If you prefer, you could use fried tofu slices, smoked tofu, mushrooms or just the vegetables. It's up to you – either way, it's really delicious.

150g (5½oz) rice noodles

1 tsp rapeseed oil

2.5cm (1in) piece of fresh root ginger, grated

1 tbsp dark soy sauce

2 tbsp vegan Thai green curry paste

1 large red pepper, sliced into julienne strips

1 carrot, sliced into julienne strips

100g (3½oz) baby corn, sliced in half on the angle

100g (3½oz) French beans, trimmed and sliced into 5cm (2in) pieces

1 spring onion, trimmed and sliced on the angle into 2.5cm (1in) pieces

small bunch coriander, stalks finely chopped, leaves separated

1–2 tbsp tamari or low-sodium light soy sauce

1 tbsp salted peanuts, crushed

1 tsp soft brown sugar

pinch of dried chilli flakes

1 lime; ½ juiced, ½ sliced into wedges

For the peanut-coated seitan

250g (9oz) seitan mock chicken pieces, drained and sliced into strips

1 tsp finely crushed peanuts

1 tbsp cornflour

First, prepare the peanut-coated seitan. Place the seitan strips in a bowl and mix well with the crushed peanuts. Dust with the cornflour and set aside.

Cook the noodles according to the packet instructions, then drain and set aside.

Heat a wok over a high heat and add the rapeseed oil. Give the oil a swirl to coat the sides of the wok, then add the ginger and stir for a few seconds to release its aroma into the oil.

Add the peanut-coated seitan and stir-fry for 1 minute. As the seitan starts to brown at the edges, add the dark soy sauce.

Loosen the Thai green curry paste with 1 tbsp water and stir it in.

Quickly follow this with all the crunchy vegetables: the red pepper, carrot, baby corn, French beans and spring onion. Cook for 1 minute, tossing all the while.

Add the rice noodles and coriander stalks, and stir well, tossing the ingredients together until all the ingredients are coated in the sauce. Season with tamari or light soy sauce and take off the heat.

Quickly mix together the crushed peanuts and brown sugar.

Divide the 'Pad Thai' between four bowls. Sprinkle over the crushed sweetened peanuts, chilli flakes and coriander leaves, then squeeze over the lime juice. Serve immediately with the lime wedges.

Garlic & Spinach Jap Cae

kcal — 474
carbs — 76.2g
protein — 9.4g
fat — 14.9g

Serves 2

25 min   5 min

This is a delicious stir-fried Korean noodle dish; it's not quite traditional, but it's my easy home-style version. This recipe uses traditional sweet potato starch noodles, which you can buy in a Korean supermarket or online. They have a great starchy, chewy texture. Gochujang, a Korean chilli bean paste, adds a spicy, smoky kick.

3 dried shiitake mushrooms

150g (5½oz) uncooked sweet potato glass noodles

toasted sesame oil, to dress the noodles

1 tbsp rapeseed oil

1 garlic clove, finely chopped

½ onion, sliced

1 carrot, sliced into julienne strips

120g (4¼oz) Chinese leaf, shredded

2 spring onions, trimmed and sliced into 2.5cm (1in) pieces

100g (3½oz) baby spinach leaves

1 tsp toasted sesame seeds, to garnish

For the sauce

1 tbsp toasted sesame oil

2 tbsp tamari or low-sodium light soy sauce

1 tbsp Shaohsing rice wine or dry sherry

1 tsp Gochujang chilli paste

½ tsp golden caster sugar

pinch of ground white pepper

Soak the dried shiitake mushrooms in hot water for 20 minutes, then drain. Remove the stalks and slice the mushrooms into 1cm (½in) slices.

Cook the noodles in boiling water for 10 minutes. Drain and rinse in cold water, then cut into lengths of about 12cm (4½in). Dress with toasted sesame oil and set aside.

To make the sauce, place the toasted sesame oil, tamari or light soy sauce, rice wine or sherry, gochujang, caster sugar and ground white pepper in a jug. Mix well to combine and set aside.

Heat a wok over a high heat until smoking, then add the rapeseed oil. Once hot, add the garlic and stir for a few seconds, then add the onion and cook, stirring, for 10 seconds. Next add the mushrooms and stir-fry for 5 seconds.

Add the carrot, Chinese leaf and spring onions and cook, tossing, for 30 seconds. Add 2 tbsp cold water at the edges of the wok to help steam the vegetables. Finally add the spinach and the cooked noodles, and toss to heat through.

Stir in the sauce and cook for another 10–15 seconds until everything is well combined and the spinach has wilted.

Remove from the heat and transfer to a serving plate. Garnish with toasted sesame seeds and serve immediately.

Spicy Chilli French Bean Mapo Tofu

Serves 2

10 min   8 min

Fine French beans tossed in a rich and spicy Sichuan Mapo Tofu, seasoned with rich and savoury chilli bean paste and drizzled with black rice vinegar for a tantalising tangy note: umami heaven, and perfect comfort food served with jasmine rice. French beans are packed with nutritional goodness: they contain vitamins A and C, and minerals including iron, calcium and magnesium; they're also low in calories and contain no saturated fat. They impart a lovely, tender, crunchy bite to the dish, adding texture and a sweet flavour.

1 tbsp cornflour

1 tbsp rapeseed oil

2 garlic cloves, finely chopped

2.5cm (1in) piece of fresh root ginger, finely grated

1 red chilli, deseeded and finely chopped

200g (7oz) fine French beans, trimmed and sliced into 1cm (½in) rounds

200g (7oz) firm tofu, drained and sliced into 1.5cm (¾in) cubes

1 tbsp chilli bean paste

1 tbsp Shaosing rice wine or dry sherry

200ml (7fl oz) cold vegetable stock

1 tbsp tamari or low-sodium light soy sauce

1 tsp Chinkiang black rice vinegar

large pinch of toasted ground Sichuan pepper, to garnish

2 spring onions, trimmed and sliced, to garnish

Before you begin, mix the cornflour with 2 tbsp water in a small bowl or cup to make a slurry. Set aside until needed.

Heat a wok over a high heat until smoking and add the rapeseed oil. Give the oil a swirl, then add the garlic, ginger and chillies and stir for a few seconds. Add the French beans, stir-fry for a few seconds, then add the tofu and cook, tossing, for a few more seconds.

Push the ingredients to one side of the wok. Add the chilli bean sauce and rice wine or sherry to the other side of the wok and cook for a few seconds.

Add the vegetable stock, stir everything to combine, and bring to the boil. Season with tamari or light soy sauce and black rice vinegar. Pour in the cornflour slurry and stir to thicken the sauce.

Transfer to a serving plate, garnish with ground Sichuan pepper and spring onions, and eat immediately.

Spicy Tempeh & Kimchi Stir-fry

kcal — 294
carbs — 19.6g
protein — 22.7g
fat — 13.8g

Serves 2

10 min 5 min

This combination of delicious, savoury tempeh paired with punchy, sour kimchi is out of this world. Traditionally it's frowned upon to stir-fry kimchi (a Korean fermented cabbage) as it might destroy all the friendly live bacteria kimchi contains, but all it needs here is a quick stir-fry. A simple and elegant dish, perfect for foodie friends.

200g (7oz) block of tempeh, sliced into 1cm (½in) strips

1 tsp dark soy sauce

pinch of sea salt flakes

pinch of freshly ground black pepper

1 tbsp cornflour

1 tbsp rapeseed oil

2.5cm (1in) piece of fresh root ginger, grated

200g (7oz) kimchi (reserve 1 tbsp of the liquid)

2 tbsp tamari or low-sodium light soy sauce

1 tsp rice vinegar

1 tsp chilli oil

2 spring onions, trimmed and sliced on the angle, to garnish

Place the tempeh strips in a bowl and season with the dark soy sauce, salt and ground black pepper. Mix well, then dust with the cornflour.

Heat a wok over a high heat and add the rapeseed oil. Once hot, add the ginger and toss for few seconds, then add the tempeh strips. Let them sear on one side for 30 seconds until brown, then turn to sear on the other side.

Add the kimchi and stir well to combine, then season with the tamari or light soy sauce, rice vinegar, chilli oil and the reserved liquid from the kimchi.

Toss gently together once more, then garnish with the spring onions and serve.

Teriyaki Tempeh with Long-stem Broccoli

kcal — 687
carbs — 108.5g
protein — 31.7g
fat — 14.5g

Serves 2

15 min   5 min

I love the Japanese teriyaki marinade: it is, arguably, one of the easiest and delicious stir-fry sauces ever invented. This dish uses chunky tempeh slices, along with long-stem broccoli, crunchy green peppers and red onions. You'll have dinner on the table in minutes.

1 tbsp rapeseed oil

2 garlic cloves, finely chopped

2.5cm (1in) piece of fresh root ginger, grated

1 small red onion, sliced into half-moon slices

200g (7oz) block of tempeh, sliced into 1cm (½in)strips

1 tbsp sake

150g (5½oz) long-stem broccoli, sliced on the angle into 2.5cm (1in) pieces

1 green pepper, sliced into julienne strips

large pinch of freshly ground black pepper

1 spring onion, trimmed and finely sliced, to garnish

pinch of black sesame seeds, to garnish

cooked jasmine rice, to serve (see page 194)

For the sauce

1 tbsp sake

2 tbsp mirin

3 tbsp tamari or low-sodium light soy sauce

2 tbsp golden syrup

In a small jug, mix together all the ingredients for the sauce and set aside.

Heat a wok over a high heat until smoking, then add the rapeseed oil. Once it's hot, add the garlic, ginger and red onion and cook, stirring, for a few seconds, until fragrant.

Add the tempeh strips and cook for 30 seconds on each side until seared and brown at the edges. Season with the sake and cook, tossing, for 2 seconds. Then add the broccoli and green pepper and stir-fry for 10 seconds more.

Pour in the sauce mixture and bring to the bubble. Continue to stir-fry until the sauce starts to reduce and you end up with a slightly sticky shine on the tempeh and peppers. Season with a large pinch of freshly ground black pepper and transfer to a serving plate.

Garnish with the spring onion and black sesame seeds. Serve immediately with jasmine rice.

5.

Warm
&
Comforting

Red-cooked Smoked Tofu, Aubergine & Potato Stew

kcal — 570
carbs — 112.0g
protein — 18.2g
fat — 8.8g

Serves 4

5 min   35 min

A frugal stew of baby aubergines and potato, cooked down in a soy liquid flavoured with star anise. I have also included Sichuan peppercorns, cinnamon, plenty of ginger, chilli and rock sugar. 'Red-cooked' is a Chinese term for this type of braised cooking technique, where the soy and sugar give a deep dark red shine to the cooking liquid as well as the ingredients.

1 tbsp rapeseed oil

1 tbsp freshly grated root ginger

1 whole dried chilli

300g (10½oz) baby aubergines, trimmed and sliced into 1.5cm (¾in) rounds

1 tbsp Sichuan peppercorns

3 star anise

2 large cinnamon sticks

5 tbsp light soy sauce

1 tbsp dark soy sauce

50g (1¾oz) rock sugar or 2–3 tbsp light brown sugar

500g (1lb 2oz) potatoes, peeled and chopped into 2cm (¾in) chunks

200g (7oz) smoked tofu, drained, rinsed in cold water and sliced into 1cm (½in) chunks

cooked jasmine rice, to serve (see page 194)

2 spring onions, trimmed and sliced into 1cm (½in) rounds, to garnish

small handful of coriander, chopped

Place a wok over a high heat until smoking, then add the rapeseed oil. Once the oil is hot, add the ginger and stir-fry for a few seconds to release its aroma. Next add the dried chilli, followed by the aubergine slices. Cook, stirring, for 2 minutes.

Add 800ml (1½ pints) water, along with the Sichuan peppercorns, star anise, cinnamon, both soy sauces and the rock sugar or light brown sugar. Bring to the boil, then reduce the heat to medium and cook for 20 minutes until the aubergine is tender.

Meanwhile, fill a separate pan with boiling water and add the potatoes. Boil them over a medium heat for 15 minutes until softened. Drain and add the potatoes to the aubergine mixture. Finally, add the tofu and cook for 10 minutes.

Garnish with the spring onions and coriander and serve with jasmine rice.

Caramelised Onion, Shiitake & Sweet Potato Congee

kcal — 409
carbs — 63.0g
protein — 9.2g
fat — 14.8g

Serves 2

15 min

35 min

This makes a warming and nourishing supper. The sweet potato lends sweetness, the brown rice some bite and the mushrooms provide a delicate umami flavour. The simple topping of soy caramelised onion makes this dish more-ish and the addition of coriander gives a mouth-watering aroma.

100g (3½oz) brown rice

1 small sweet potato, peeled and diced into 1cm (½in) cubes

½ tsp + ½ tbsp vegetable bouillon powder

1 tbsp rapeseed oil

2 garlic cloves, finely chopped

1 red chilli, deseeded and finely chopped

½ carrot, finely diced

6 fresh shiitake mushrooms, sliced

1–2 tbsp tamari or low-sodium light soy sauce

pinch of freshly ground black pepper, plus extra to serve

1 tsp toasted sesame oil

handful of shredded pak choi leaves

small bunch of coriander, leaves separated and stalks finely chopped, to garnish

For the soy caramelised onion

1 tbsp rapeseed oil

1 red onion, sliced into half-moon slices

large pinch of golden caster sugar

1 tbsp tamari or low-sodium light soy sauce

Wash the brown rice well in a colander until the water runs clear. Place the rinsed rice in a medium saucepan. Add the sweet potato cubes and ½ tsp vegetable bouillon powder and cover with 250ml (9fl oz) cold water. Place over a medium heat and bring to the boil. Once boiling, cover with a tight-fitting lid, reduce the heat to low and let simmer for 20 minutes. Once cooked, remove the lid and fluff the grains with a fork.

To make the soy caramelised onion, heat a wok over a medium heat until slightly smoking, then add the rapeseed oil. Once hot, add the red onion slices and season with the sugar. Cook for 2–3 minutes until softened and caramelised. Stir through the tamari or light soy sauce. Transfer to small plate and set aside.

Give the wok a quick rinse, then return it to the heat. Add the rapeseed oil, followed by the garlic and chilli. Stir-fry for a few seconds, then add the carrot and stir-fry for 1–2 minutes.

Tip in the cooked brown rice and sweet potato, then pour in 500ml (18fl oz) boiling water. Add the remaining ½ tbsp bouillon powder and bring back to the boil. Cook over a medium heat for 8 minutes.

Add the shiitake mushrooms and cook for 1 minute, then add the tamari or light soy sauce, along with the black pepper and sesame oil. Stir through the shredded pak choi and wilt for 20 seconds.

Divide the congee between two bowls, top each portion with some soy caramelised onions and garnish with coriander. Grind over some more black pepper to taste and serve.

Lemon & Ginger Breaded Cauliflower 'Cutlets'

kcal — 770
carbs — 149.4g
protein — 16.2g
fat — 16.2g

Serves 2

20 min

12–15 min

Cauliflower steaks are delicious when grilled, roasted or pan-fried, but I love them breaded, shallow-fried and served with a lemon sauce. Tasty and satisfying, these cutlets are perfect with steamed vegetables and jasmine rice.

2 cauliflower 'steaks', cut from a head sliced across the bulb, with stalk and florets intact

50g (1¾oz) plain flour

100ml (3½fl oz) aquafaba

50g (1¾oz) dried breadcrumbs

1 spring onion, trimmed and finely chopped

rapeseed oil, for shallow-frying

sea salt and freshly ground black pepper

shichimi togarashi pepper flakes, to garnish

cooked jasmine rice (see page 194) and steamed vegetables, to serve

For the lemon & ginger sauce

1 tbsp cornflour

1 tbsp rapeseed oil

1 tsp freshly grated root ginger

juice of 2 lemons

3 tbsp golden syrup

pinch of Chinese five spice

50ml (2fl oz) vegetable stock

1 tbsp tamari or low-sodium light soy sauce

small handful of finely chopped chives

Season the cauliflower steaks with salt and pepper.

Place the flour, aquafaba and breadcrumbs in three separate dishes. Add the spring onion to the aquafaba.

One at a time, dip the cauliflower steaks into the flour, covering and coating well, then into the aquafaba, trying to collect as much of the spring onion as possible. Finally, dip into the breadcrumbs and coat well.

Heat a shallow pan over a medium heat and add rapeseed oil to a depth of about 0.5cm (¼in). Heat the oil to 160°C (325°F). Add the cutlets and shallow-fry, cooking for 2 minutes on each side until the breadcrumbs are golden and the cutlets are cooked but still have a bite. Remove from the heat and keep warm in a low oven.

To make the sauce, begin by mixing the cornflour with 2 tbsp water in a small bowl or cup to make a slurry. Set aside until needed.

Heat a wok over a medium heat until slightly smoking, then add the rapeseed oil. Once hot, add the ginger and fry for a few seconds, then add the lemon juice, golden syrup, Chinese five spice, vegetable stock and tamari or light soy sauce, and bring to the bubble. Stir in the cornflour slurry and stir to thicken. Finally, add the finely chopped chives.

Remove the cauliflower cutlets from the oven. Sprinkle some shichimi togarashi pepper flakes over each cutlet. Place each cutlet on a plate with some cooked jasmine rice and steamed veg of your choice, then spoon over the sauce and serve immediately.

Crispy Mushroom Spring Onion Pancakes

kcal — 550
carbs — 85.5g
protein — 11.5g
fat — 20.4g

Serves 6 as a side
(makes 6 pancakes)

30 min · 25 min

These *jian bing* pancakes make a perfect fun treat for family and friends. Everyone can make and assemble their own, so they're great for party food! They are comforting and delicious.

250g (9oz) shimeji mushrooms, separated

2 tbsp vegetarian mushroom sauce

80g (2¾oz) plain flour

125ml (4fl oz) aquafaba

80g (2¾oz) breadcrumbs

dried chilli flakes, to taste

1 tsp Chinese five spice

olive oil spray

sea salt and ground white pepper

For the pancakes

365g (12¾oz) plain flour, plus 2 tbsp extra for dusting

75g (2¾oz) strong bread flour

½ tsp salt

3 tbsp rapeseed oil

1 tbsp toasted sesame oil

½ tsp ground white pepper

½ tsp ground black pepper

1½ tsp ground sea salt

4 spring onions, trimmed and finely chopped

6 tsp rapeseed oil, for frying

To serve

3 tbsp vegan mayonnaise

1 tbsp sriracha

6 tsp vegetarian mushroom sauce

1 tsp Chiu Chow chilli oil (optional, for added spice)

4 tbsp toasted sesame seeds

2 spring onions, trimmed and finely sliced

handful of freshly chopped coriander

2 red chillies, sliced on the angle

Preheat the oven to 180°C/160°C fan/350°F/Gas Mark 4.

Place the mushrooms in a bowl and pour over the mushroom sauce. Mix well and leave to marinate for 15 minutes.

Place the flour, aquafaba and breadcrumbs in three separate dishes. Season the breadcrumbs with salt, ground white pepper, dried chilli flakes and Chinese five spice.

Dip the mushrooms first into the flour, covering and coating well, then into the aquafaba. Finally, dip into the breadcrumbs and coat well. Place the breadcrumb-covered mushrooms on a roasting tray, spray with the olive oil spray and roast for 10–12 minutes.

Meanwhile, make the spring onion pancakes. In a large bowl, mix together the plain flour, the strong bread flour and the salt. Add 200ml (7fl oz) boiling water and mix into a dough. Add 150ml (5fl oz) cold water and knead into a smooth dough. Set aside.

Heat the 3 tbsp rapeseed oil and 1 tbsp of sesame oil in a small saucepan over a medium heat. Add the white pepper, black pepper and salt. Remove from the heat.

Lightly dust your work surface with 1 tbsp of flour. Roll out the dough into a flat circle and spread the seasoned oil on to it, taking care not to spread the oil right to the edges. Scatter the spring onions onto the dough, then scatter the remaining 1 tbsp of plain flour over the top.

Cut the dough into eight segments, stopping about 2cm (¾in) from the centre of the dough so that each section is still attached. Take one section and fold it towards the centre of the circle, then repeat with the remaining sections. Roll the dough out again and repeat this circular folding process. This creates stretchy, chewy layers in the pancake.

Roll out the dough once again, this time into a rectangle, then roll that into a long Swiss-roll shape; it should be about 10cm (4in) wide. Divide this into six pieces. Flatten each piece with your palm and use your hands or a rolling pin to stretch the dough into a circle. You should end up with six small–medium pancakes.

Heat a wok or frying pan over a medium heat. Add some rapeseed oil and swirl it up the sides of the pan (alternatively, you can brush each pancake on both sides with 1 tsp rapeseed oil to ensure even cooking). Add 2–3 pancakes to the pan at a time and cook until golden-brown, turning halfway. Repeat until all the pancakes are cooked. Cover with foil and keep warm in the oven until ready to serve.

Mix together the vegan mayonnaise and sriracha in a small bowl.

When you're ready to serve, spread 1 tsp vegetarian mushroom sauce on each pancake, and place some of the crispy roasted mushrooms on top. Drizzle over the sriracha-vegan mayonnaise and Chiu Chow chilli oil, if using. Sprinkle over some toasted sesame seeds, spring onions, coriander and freshly sliced chilli. Eat immediately.

Thai-style Roasted Sweet Chilli Sprouts with Creamy Coconut Noodles

kcal — 559
carbs — 54.4g
protein — 11.9g
fat — 32.7g

Serves 4

5 min   38 min

This is a super delicious dish with lots of flavours and textures going on: it's sweet, spicy, nutty and creamy. It's comforting on so many levels, and I love the way it really makes the veg the star of the show.

200g (7oz) dried wheat-flour noodles

1 tbsp toasted sesame oil

2 garlic cloves, roughly chopped

3 small shallots, roughly chopped

2 lemongrass stalks, roughly chopped

1 tbsp rapeseed oil

1 tbsp tamari or low-sodium light soy sauce

400ml (14fl oz) can coconut milk

small handful of chopped coriander, to garnish

For the roasted sweet chilli sprouts

200g (7oz) Brussels sprouts, trimmed

1 tbsp rapeseed oil

1 tsp vegan Thai red curry paste

2 tbsp sweet chilli sauce

1 tbsp golden syrup

50g (1¾oz) raw unsalted cashew nuts

Preheat the oven to 180°C/160°C fan/350°F/Gas Mark 4.

Begin by making the sprouts. Heat a wok and fill it with water. Bring to the boil and add the Brussels sprouts. Cook for 3 minutes, until tender but still al dente. Drain and rinse the sprouts under the cold tap.

Transfer the sprouts to a roasting tray. Add the rapeseed oil, Thai red curry paste, sweet chilli sauce and golden syrup and roast for 15 minutes. Add the cashew nuts and return the tray to the oven to roast for another 5 minutes until golden.

Meanwhile, cook the noodles according to the packet instructions and rinse in cold water. Drain and drizzle over the toasted sesame oil to prevent them from sticking together.

In a food processor, blitz together the garlic, shallots and lemongrass to form a paste.

Heat a wok over a high heat until smoking, then add the rapeseed oil. Once hot, add the garlic, shallot and lemongrass paste and fry for a few seconds, then add the Thai red curry paste and cook, stirring, for a few seconds more.

Stir in the tamari or light soy sauce followed by the coconut milk. Cook for 12 minutes until the liquid has turned a dark red colour. Add the drained noodles and toss to coat well.

To serve, divide the creamy noodles between four bowls and top with the roasted sprouts. Garnish with coriander and serve immediately.

Thai Green Curry Courgette Fried Rice

kcal — 425
carbs — 63.0g
protein — 10.8g
fat — 15.8g

Serves 2

20 min   7–8 min

This recipe was born because I ran out of coconut milk. I didn't have enough to make a full curry, so I opted for a fried rice instead. It was super yum – I love it when a veggie plan comes together!

1 tbsp rapeseed oil

2.5cm (1in) piece of fresh root ginger, grated

1 green chilli, deseeded and finely chopped

1 tbsp vegan Thai green curry paste

2 courgettes, sliced into 0.5cm (¼in) rounds

225g (8oz) can whole water chestnuts, drained

handful of mangetout

300g (10½oz) cooked jasmine rice (see page 194)

100ml (3½fl oz) coconut milk (see tip on page 67)

1 tsp dark soy sauce

1–2 tbsp tamari or low-sodium light soy sauce

pinch of freshly ground black pepper

handful of coriander, stalks finely chopped and leaves separated

1 spring onion, trimmed and finely sliced

2 lime wedges, to serve

Heat a wok over a high heat until smoking, then add the rapeseed oil. Once hot, add the ginger, chilli and green curry paste and cook, stirring, for a few seconds. Then add the courgettes and stir-fry for 1 minute.

Add the water chestnuts and mangetout and stir-fry for another minute. Tip in the cooked rice and toss well to combine. Add the coconut milk, dark soy sauce, tamari or light soy sauce and black pepper. Keep cooking, stirring all the while, until the rice is heated through. Toss through the coriander stalks.

Divide the fried rice between two plates. Sprinkle over the spring onion and coriander leaves, and serve with lime wedges, for squeezing.

Veggie Spicy Singapore-style Noodles

kcal — 463
carbs — 62.0g
protein — 14.9g
fat — 18.2g

Serves 2

15 min   6 min

I like to cheat and buy ready-cooked vermicelli rice noodles when I know I am busy as they make this dish even more speedy. With a few fresh ingredients combined with store-cupboard basics, this dish never fails to deliver on speed, flavour and comfort.

1 tbsp rapeseed oil

2 garlic cloves, peeled and finely chopped

2.5cm (1in) piece of fresh root ginger, grated

2 red chillies, deseeded and finely chopped

4 fresh shiitake mushrooms, cut into 0.5cm (¼in) slices

100g (3½oz) smoked tofu, drained, rinsed in cold water and sliced into julienne strips

1 tsp ground turmeric

1 tbsp Shaohsing rice wine or dry sherry

350g (12oz) ready-cooked vermicelli rice noodles

2 spring onions, trimmed and finely sliced on the angle

2 tbsp tamari or low-sodium light soy sauce

1 tbsp vegetarian mushroom sauce

½ tsp dried chilli flakes

pinch of freshly ground white pepper

1 tbsp toasted sesame oil

small handful of beansprouts, washed

small handful of coriander leaves, to garnish

Heat a wok over a high heat until smoking and add the rapeseed oil. Once hot, add the garlic, ginger and red chillies and cook for a few seconds, then add the mushrooms and smoked tofu and toss together for 20 seconds.

Add the turmeric and cook for another 10 seconds, then add the rice wine or sherry around the edges of the wok. Add the rice noodles and spring onions and toss for 20 seconds, ensuring that all the noodles are coated in the turmeric, and the dish is uniform in colour.

Add a small dash of water around the edges of the wok to help create some steam, then stir in the tamari or light soy sauce and vegetarian mushroom sauce and toss for 1 minute to combine. Sprinkle over the dried chilli and ground white pepper and stir in the toasted sesame oil. Add the beansprouts and toss together well to wilt for 30 seconds.

Transfer to a serving plate, garnish with fresh coriander and serve immediately.

Smoked Tofu & Broccoli Korean-style Ram-don

kcal — 552
carbs — 57.9g
protein — 30.2g
fat — 21.9g

Serves 4

15 min   9 min

This is inspired by the beef ram-don in the Korean movie *Parasite*. I wanted to make a vegan version using chunky smoked tofu, mushrooms and long-stem broccoli. The result is a more-ish, umami-rich, addictively spicy noodle dish. To make the dish speedier, I place the aromatics (garlic, ginger, shallots and chilli) in a food processor and then just add them to the wok.

200g (7oz) dried ramen or udon noodles

1 tbsp toasted sesame oil

2 garlic cloves

2.5cm (1in) piece of fresh root ginger, peeled

3 shallots

2 red chillies, deseeded

1 tbsp cornflour

1 tbsp rapeseed oil

200g (7oz) smoked tofu, drained, rinsed in cold water and sliced into 2cm (¾in) cubes

400g (14oz) firm tofu, drained and sliced into 2cm (¾in) cubes

200g (7oz) fresh shiitake mushrooms

1 tbsp Shaohsing rice wine

2 tbsp dark soy sauce

150g (5½oz) long-stem broccoli, florets sliced lengthwise and stalks sliced into 0.5cm (¼in) rounds

2 tbsp vegetarian mushroom sauce

1 tbsp clear rice vinegar

1 tbsp tamari or low-sodium light soy sauce

2 spring onions, trimmed and finely sliced on the angle into 1cm (½in) slices

Noodle seasoning (per bowl)

1 tsp dark soy sauce and Chiu Chow chilli oil

1 tbsp each tahini and sweet chilli sauce

sprinkle of shichimi togarashi pepper flakes

Cook the noodles according to the packet instructions. Rinse under cold water and drain well, then drizzle over the toasted sesame oil to prevent them from sticking together. Set aside in the colander until needed.

Place the garlic, ginger, shallots and red chillies in a small food processor and blitz to form a paste.

Mix the cornflour with 2 tbsp water in a small bowl or cup to make a slurry. Set aside until needed.

Heat a wok over a high heat until smoking and add the rapeseed oil. Once hot, add the aromatic paste and cook, stirring, for a few seconds until fragrant. Add both kinds of tofu and the mushrooms. Season with the rice wine and dark soy sauce and toss together well for 1–2 minutes until all the ingredients are coated.

Add the broccoli and cook, tossing, for 1 minute. Stir in the mushroom sauce, rice vinegar and tamari or light soy sauce. Pour in the cornflour slurry to thicken the cooking juices in the wok, and toss to mix well.

Pour some boiling water over the noodles in the colander to reheat them, then divide them between four bowls.

Place a ladleful of the tofu, mushroom and broccoli mixture on one side of the noodles in each bowl, and top with the sliced spring onion. Dress the noodles by drizzling over the dark soy sauce, Chiu Chow chilli oil, tahini and sweet chilli sauce, followed by a generous sprinkle of shichimi togarashi pepper flakes. Serve immediately.

Warm & Comforting

Crispy Sweet Chilli Tofu & Water Chestnuts

kcal — 484
carbs — 62.9g
protein — 13.5g
fat — 21.3g

Serves 4 as a side

15 min   10 min

If you don't like tofu, this dish will be sure to change your mind! Fried golden pieces of tofu are wokked up in a sweet and sour chilli sauce with crunchy water chestnuts. This is heavenly mopped up with jasmine rice: the ultimate Friday night fake-away. If you're still not convinced about tofu, you can use mushrooms or seitan.

400g (14oz) firm tofu, drained, patted completely dry and sliced into 1.5cm (¾in) cubes

pinch of sea salt

pinch of ground white pepper

160ml (5½fl oz) aquafaba

4 tbsp cornflour

vegetable oil, for frying

cooked jasmine rice, to serve (see page 194)

For the sweet chilli sauce

1 tsp rapeseed oil

3 garlic cloves, finely chopped

2.5cm (1in) piece of fresh root ginger, grated

1 red chilli, deseeded and finely chopped

3 tbsp sweet chilli sauce

1 tbsp tamari or low-sodium light soy sauce

juice of 1 lime

225g (8oz) can sliced water chestnuts, drained

1 spring onion, trimmed and finely sliced

small handful of freshly chopped coriander

In a bowl, season the tofu cubes with the salt and ground white pepper.

In a separate bowl, combine the aquafaba and cornflour to make a batter.

Heat a wok over a high heat until smoking and fill it one-third full with vegetable oil. Heat the oil to 180°C (350°F), or until a cube of bread turns golden-brown in 15 seconds and floats to the surface.

Dip a piece of tofu in the batter and then gently drop into the oil. Make sure you use a frying shield or wok lid should the oil splutter or splash back. Continue with the rest of the tofu pieces, gently adding them to the oil in the wok. Cook for 5 minutes until the tofu pieces are golden and crispy. Lift out using a stainless steel spider strainer or tongs and place on a plate lined with kitchen paper to drain.

Pour the remaining oil from the wok into a heatproof container. Leave to cool before discarding the oil.

To make the sauce, reheat the wok on a high heat until smoking, then add 1 tsp rapeseed oil. Once hot, add the garlic, ginger and chilli and stir-fry for a few seconds. Add the sweet chilli sauce, tamari or light soy sauce and lime juice. Add the water chestnuts and bring to the bubble.

Once the sauce is bubbling, add the golden tofu cubes to the wok. Toss quickly and gently, coating all the pieces in the sauce. Turn out on to a plate and sprinkle over some chopped coriander. Eat immediately with jasmine rice.

Veggie Ants Climbing Trees

kcal — 305
carbs — 44.0g
protein — 14.9g
fat — 8.4g

Serves 4 as a starter
or side

20 min   7 min

This is a Sichuan street-food dish. The unusual name came about because the small pieces of minced soy on the noodles look like ants climbing trees, with the noodles being the trees' branches. The trick is to use minced soy and vegetarian mushroom sauce for a hit of umami, along with small pieces of rehydrated dried Chinese mushrooms for a heartier bite. This dish is super satisfying to eat!

125g (4½oz) dehydrated minced soy

210ml (7¼fl oz) boiling water or hot vegetable stock

5 large dried Chinese mushrooms

150g (5½oz) dried mung bean noodles

2 tbsp rapeseed oil

2 garlic cloves, finely chopped

1 tbsp freshly grated root ginger

1 red chilli, deseeded and finely chopped

1 tbsp Shaohsing rice wine or dry sherry

1 tbsp vegetarian mushroom sauce

1 tbsp dark soy sauce

1 tbsp chilli bean paste

200ml (7fl oz) hot vegetable stock

1 tsp pure sesame oil

2 large spring onions, trimmed and finely chopped

To rehydrate the minced soy, add the hot water or stock and leave to stand for 5 minutes.

Place the mushrooms in a bowl and cover with hot water. Leave to soak for 20 minutes, then drain. Remove the stalks and finely dice the mushrooms.

At the same time, place the mung bean noodles in a large bowl and soak in hot water for 10 minutes. Drain and set aside until needed.

Heat a wok over a high heat until smoking, then add the rapeseed oil. Once hot, add the garlic, ginger and chilli and stir-fry for a few seconds, then add the minced soy and mushrooms and stir-fry for 2–3 minutes until browned at the edges.

Add the rice wine or sherry, mushroom sauce, soy sauce and chilli bean paste and mix well. Stir in the hot stock and bring to the boil, then add the drained noodles and stir well.

Season with the sesame oil, add the spring onions, toss to combine and serve immediately.

Hawaiian Sticky Mushroom & Pineapple Fried Rice

kcal — 580
carbs — 101.5g
protein — 16.6g
fat — 14.7g

Serves 2

15 min   5 min

Fresh king trumpet mushrooms, wok-fried in tamari, sweet chilli and sriracha and served with chickpeas, sweetcorn and carrots in a hollowed-out pineapple! Pineapples are a super fruit: high in vitamin C, they defend your body from free radicals and help digestion by cleaning the body's organs and blood. They also increase your energy intake, boost your metabolism and nourish your skin and hair from the inside. Serve with Chiu Chow chilli oil for a spicy kick.

1 tbsp rapeseed oil

2.5cm (1in) piece of fresh root ginger, finely grated

100g (3½oz) carrots, diced

200g (7oz) can sweetcorn, drained

400g (14oz) can chickpeas, drained and rinsed well

200g (7oz) fresh king trumpet mushrooms, sliced into strips

300g (10½oz) cooked jasmine rice (see page 194)

1 tbsp dark soy sauce

2 tbsp sweet chilli sauce

1 tsp sriracha

2 tbsp tamari or low-sodium light soy sauce

150g (5½oz) fresh pineapple, diced (if you are using flesh from a whole pineapple, you can keep the hollowed-out shell, to serve)

large pinch of ground white pepper

1 tsp toasted sesame oil

To serve

1 red chilli, deseeded and finely chopped

small handful of freshly chopped chives

1 tsp Chiu Chow chilli oil

Heat a wok over a high heat until smoking, then add the rapeseed oil. Once hot, give the oil a swirl, then add the ginger and stir-fry for a few seconds. Add the carrots and cook for a few seconds, then add the sweetcorn, chickpeas and mushrooms and cook, tossing, for less than 1 minute. Add the cooked jasmine rice and use your spoon to gently break down the rice in the wok.

Add the dark soy sauce, sweet chilli sauce, sriracha and tamari or light soy sauce and toss to mix well. Add the pineapple and stir to combine.

Now add the ground white pepper and toasted sesame oil. Spoon the mixture out of the wok and into a hollowed-out pineapple, if using. Sprinkle over the chopped chives and chilli, and serve with Chiu Chow chilli oil on the side.

Chilli Bean Smoked Tofu with Noodles

kcal — 405
carbs — 41.2g
protein — 23.9g
fat — 16.5g

Serves 4 as a starter

10 min   25 min

This 'meaty' tasting dish is inspired by one of my favourite dishes, found in the narrow alleyways of Shanghai at a local home kitchen called Chang Jiao Mian Dian. This dish is full of rich umami flavours and so delicious that it will leave you wanting seconds.

400g (14oz) smoked tofu, drained, rinsed in cold water and sliced into 1cm (½in) cubes

large pinch of sea salt

large pinch of freshly ground black pepper

2 tbsp rapeseed oil

1 large onion, finely diced

3 garlic cloves, finely chopped

2.5cm (1in) piece of fresh root ginger, grated

2 celery sticks, cut into 0.5cm (¼in) slices

2 carrots, cut into 0.5cm (¼in) slices on the angle

1 tbsp chilli bean paste

1 tbsp tamari or low-sodium light soy sauce

1 tsp dark soy sauce

1 tbsp vegetarian mushroom sauce

1 tbsp Shaohsing rice wine or dry sherry

1 litre (1¾ pints) vegetable stock

1 bay leaf

1 star anise

150g (5½oz) dried wide knife-cut noodles or flat udon noodles

freshly chopped coriander

For the dipping sauce

1 red chilli, finely sliced on a deep angle

1 tbsp tamari or low-sodium light soy sauce

Season the smoked tofu with salt and ground black pepper.

Heat a wok over a high heat until smoking, then add 1 tbsp rapeseed oil. Once hot, add the smoked tofu pieces and sear all over for 2 minutes until browned. Transfer the tofu pieces to a plate and set aside.

Reduce the heat to medium and add the remaining tbsp of rapeseed oil. Once hot, add the onion and fry until translucent, then add the garlic, ginger, celery and carrots and cook for 3 minutes.

Stir in the chilli bean paste, tamari or light soy sauce, dark soy sauce, mushroom sauce and rice wine or sherry. Add the stock, along with the bay leaf and star anise. Return the smoked tofu to the wok. Cover with the lid and cook on a medium–low heat for 20 minutes.

Meanwhile, cook the noodles according to the packet instructions. Once the tofu mixture has been cooking for 20 minutes, add the noodles to the wok and stir together well.

To make the dipping sauce, place the sliced chilli in a small bowl and add the tamari or light soy sauce.

To serve, ladle the noodles and tofu into bowls, sprinkle with the coriander stalks and leaves and serve alongside the dipping sauce.

Hoisin Seitan Rice Noodles

kcal — 423
carbs — 54.4g
protein — 19.9g
fat — 14.2g

Serves 2

3 min   16 min

Seitan pieces are wokked up in a sweet, salty Chinese barbecue-style Hoisin sauce alongside carrots and shiitake mushrooms with ginger and dark soy sauce, served on a bed of seasoned rice noodles. This is salty, sweet, spicy and sour – all my favourite flavours in one dish! If you don't like seitan, try dried Chinese mushrooms, smoked tofu or minced soy.

70g (2½oz) beansprouts

100g (3½oz) dried flat rice noodles

1 tsp toasted sesame oil

1 tbsp rapeseed oil

2.5cm (1in) fresh root ginger, grated

1 carrot, finely diced

4 fresh shiitake mushrooms, finely diced

100g (3½oz) seitan mock chicken pieces, finely chopped

1 tbsp hoisin sauce

1 tsp dark soy sauce

1 tbsp Shaohsing rice wine or dry sherry

To serve

1 tbsp tahini

1 tsp tamari or low-sodium light soy sauce

1 tsp Chinkiang black rice vinegar

1 tsp Chiu Chow chilli oil

2 spring onions, trimmed and finely sliced

In a saucepan over a medium heat, bring 1 litre (1¾ pints) water to the boil. Add the beansprouts for 10 seconds, blanching them, then lift out using a slotted spoon and set aside. To the same saucepan of boiling water, add the dried rice noodles and cook for 10–12 minutes (or according to the packet instructions) until al dente, then drain under cold water. Drizzle over the toasted sesame oil and toss together to prevent the noodles from sticking.

Heat a wok over a high heat until smoking, then add the rapeseed oil. Once hot, add the ginger and stir-fry for a few seconds. Next add the carrots, stir-frying for 1 minute, then the shiitake mushrooms, followed by the seitan pieces. Cook for 1 minute, until browning at the edges.

Pour in the hoisin sauce and cook, stirring, for 30 seconds. Season with the dark soy sauce and rice wine or sherry and toss well together.

To serve, place the drained noodles on a serving plate and top with the beansprouts, followed by the seitan mixture. Drizzle over the tahini, tamari or light soy sauce, black rice vinegar and Chiu Chow chilli oil. Scatter over the finely chopped spring onions and serve immediately. Before eating, mix well so all the flavours marry together.

Warm & Comforting

Shredded Seitan 'Duck' Fried Rice

kcal — 446
carbs — 74.9g
protein — 19.0g
fat — 9.0g

Serves 4 as a side

20 min   30 min

This extravagant fried rice will leave you craving more. The mock duck is delicious on its own, but here it adds a spiced savoury meatiness to the rice.

400g (14oz) seitan mock duck, drained and finely sliced

250g (9oz) short-grain sushi rice, rinsed well

½ tsp vegetable bouillon powder

1 tbsp rapeseed oil

2 garlic cloves, finely grated

1 red chilli, deseeded and finely chopped

1 spring onion, trimmed and finely chopped

¼ white cabbage, finely shredded

1 tbsp Shaohsing rice wine

2 tbsp vegetarian mushroom sauce

1 tbsp tamari or low-sodium light soy sauce

1 tsp toasted sesame oil

pinch of ground white pepper

For the marinade

2 garlic cloves, finely grated

2.5cm (1in) piece of fresh root ginger, finely grated

1 tbsp Shaohsing rice wine or dry sherry

1 tsp Chinese five spice

2 tbsp maple or golden syrup

2 tbsp hoisin sauce

1 tbsp chilli bean sauce

1 tbsp dark soy sauce

To garnish

toasted pine nuts, coriander leaves and Chiu Chow chilli oil

Place the mock duck pieces in a dish and add all the ingredients of the marinade. Cover and leave to marinate for at least 20 minutes.

Meanwhile, cook the sushi rice. Place the washed rice in a medium-sized saucepan. Add the vegetable bouillon powder and 450ml (16fl oz) water and place over a medium heat. Bring to the boil, then reduce the heat to low and place a lid on the saucepan. Cook, covered, on this low heat for 15 minutes. Remove the lid, fluff up the rice and transfer to a tray to cool for 10–15 minutes at room temperature.

Preheat the oven to 180°C/160°C/350°F/Gas Mark 4. When the mock duck has finished marinating, transfer the mock duck (and all the marinade) into a roasting tray lined with baking paper. Roast for 10 minutes until slightly caramelised at the edges, then remove from the oven and set aside to rest. Slice into fine pieces like julienne strips.

Heat a wok over a high heat until smoking, then add the rapeseed oil. Once hot, add the chilli and spring onion and stir-fry for a few seconds, then add the white cabbage and cook, tossing, for 30 seconds until wilted.

Add the rice wine, followed by the cooked sushi rice and the roasted mock duck. Stir in the mushroom sauce and tamari or light soy sauce and keep cooking, stirring all the time, until all the ingredients are combined well. Season with toasted sesame oil and ground white pepper.

Garnish with a scattering of toasted pine nuts and coriander leaves and a drizzling of Chiu Chow chilli oil, and serve immediately.

Warm & Comforting

Veggie Ball Noodle Soup

kcal — 393
carbs — 49.0g
protein — 11.0g
fat — 18.2g

Serves 4
(makes 12 balls)

15 min   15 min

This is inspired by my love of Hong Kong-style fish ball noodle soup. I decided to make a vegan version of the balls using mushrooms and tofu and the results are delish. Enjoy!

500ml (18fl oz) vegetable oil

1.5 litres (2¾ pints) vegetable stock

200g (7oz) Chinese leaf, sliced into 2.5cm (1in) strips

200g (7oz) ready-to-eat vermicelli rice noodles

pinch of sea salt flakes

pinch of ground white pepper

1 tbsp tamari or low-sodium light soy sauce

1 tsp toasted sesame oil

1 tsp Chiu Chow chilli oil, to serve

finely chopped chives, to serve

freshly chopped coriander leaves, to serve

For the veggie balls

200g (7oz) fresh firm tofu

100g (3½oz) dried Chinese mushrooms, soaked in hot water for 20 minutes, drained and finely chopped

50g (1¾oz) tinned chickpeas, drained, aquafaba reserved (see below)

1 tbsp freshly grated fresh root ginger

1 spring onion, trimmed and finely chopped

1 tsp Shaohsing rice wine or dry sherry

50g (1¾oz) cornflour

1 tsp vegetarian mushroom sauce

pinch of sea salt flakes

pinch of ground white pepper

125ml (4fl oz) aquafaba

1 tbsp coriander stalks, finely chopped

Place all the ingredients for the veggie balls (except the aquafaba and coriander stalks) in a food processor and blend well until airy and light. Slowly pour in the aquafaba and blitz well. Sprinkle over the finely chopped coriander stalks and mix again.

Use 2 tablespoons to shape the mixture into approximately 12 balls.

Heat a wok over a high heat until smoking and add the vegetable oil. Heat the oil to 180°C (350°F). Using a spider strainer or slotted metal spoon, carefully lower each veggie ball into the oil. Spoon some of the oil over them to brown them all over. When the balls have all turned golden-brown, remove carefully and place on a heatproof plate lined with kitchen paper. For crispy veggie balls, you can re-fry them twice by reusing the oil.

Fill a large stock pot with the vegetable stock and bring to a simmer over a medium heat. Add the Chinese leaf and cook for 1 minute, then add the vermicelli rice noodles. Season with the sea salt and ground white pepper.

Reduce the heat to medium and gently add the veggie balls. Cook for 2–3 minutes until the balls float to the surface.

Season with tamari or light soy sauce and toasted sesame oil and bring to the boil.

Divide the noodles between four bowls, ladle over the stock and Chinese leaves, and place six veggie balls in each bowl. Drizzle over the Chiu Chow chilli oil and sprinkle over the finely chopped chives and coriander leaves. Serve immediately.

Spicy Sweet Potato & Water Chestnut Fried Rice

Serves 2

15 min   7 min

Sweet potato, fragrant rice and crunchy, nutty water chestnuts in a spicy, sweet sauce makes this a more-ish and quick mid-week supper. For a meatier bite, you have the option of adding fresh shiitake mushrooms.

1 tbsp rapeseed oil

2 small garlic cloves, finely chopped

2.5cm (1in) piece of fresh root ginger, finely grated

1 large red cayenne chilli, deseeded and sliced

150g (5½oz) sweet potatoes, peeled and diced into 0.5cm (¼in) cubes

225g (8oz) can sliced water chestnuts, drained

1 pak choi, shredded

1 tbsp Shaohsing rice wine or dry sherry

300g (10½oz) cooked jasmine rice (see page 194)

100g (3½oz) fresh shiitake mushrooms, sliced (optional)

For the Sichuan spicy sauce

1 tbsp chilli bean paste

2 tbsp Chinkiang black rice vinegar

1 tbsp tamari or low-sodium light soy sauce

1 tsp soft brown sugar

1 tsp toasted sesame oil

50ml (2fl oz) cold water

Place all the ingredients for the Sichuan spicy sauce in a bowl. Mix well and set aside.

Heat a wok over a high heat until smoking, then add the rapeseed oil. Once hot, add the garlic, ginger and chilli and stir-fry for a few seconds. Then add the sweet potato cubes, adding a few drops of water to create some steam to soften and cook them. Cook for 2–3 minutes until the sweet potatoes have softened but still have a bite.

Add the water chestnuts and pak choi, followed by the rice wine or sherry. Cook, tossing, for 1 minute.

Add the cooked jasmine rice to the wok (along with the mushrooms, if using) and toss everything together. Pour in the Sichuan spicy sauce and cook, tossing, for 2 minutes until the sauce has coated the rice and other ingredients. Serve immediately.

Spicy Chickpea Noodle Soup

kcal — 601
carbs — 107.6g
protein — 26.4g
fat — 7.6g

Serves 2

5 min   30 min

The flavours in this soup are inspired by beef noodle broths. The depth of flavour comes from boiling the umami-rich tomatoes, soy and daikon. This makes a perfect, quick, satisfying dinner that is comforting on a cold winter's night.

200g (7oz) dried flat wheat-flour udon noodles

1 tsp toasted sesame oil

120g (4¼oz) baby pak choi

freshly chopped coriander, to garnish

For the broth

4 large garlic cloves, peeled and lightly crushed

2.5cm (1in) piece of fresh root ginger, sliced into thirds

3 shallots, peeled

1 red chilli, deseeded and finely chopped

170g (6oz) carrots, chopped into 2.5cm (1in) rounds

150g (5½oz) large tomatoes, quartered

200g (7oz) daikon, sliced into 2.5cm (1in) chunks

2 star anise

large pinch of sea salt flakes

400g (14oz) can chickpeas, drained and rinsed

1 tbsp dark soy sauce

1 tbsp tamari or low-sodium light soy sauce

1 tbsp chilli bean paste

Heat 1 litre (1¾ pints) water in a large stockpot over a medium heat. Add all of the broth ingredients and simmer, covered, for 30 minutes.

Five minutes before the broth will be ready, bring a large saucepan of water to the boil in a separate saucepan. Add the udon noodles and boil for 5 minutes until al dente. Drain and rinse under cold water, then drizzle over the toasted sesame oil to prevent the noodles from sticking together.

Meanwhile, bring 600ml (20fl oz) water to the boil in a large pot. Add the baby pak choi and blanch for 5 seconds, then drain and plunge into iced water to keep the colour. Set aside.

To serve, divide the noodles between two large bowls, then pour 3–4 ladles of the broth and vegetables into each bowl. Decorate with 1–2 pieces of blanched pak choi per bowl and garnish with fresh coriander. Serve immediately.

Satay Seitan
with Courgetti Noodles

kcal — 591
carbs — 31.5g
protein — 41.0g
fat — 32.7g

Serves 2

15 min   15 min

This is one of my favourite recipes. It is inspired by my love of Indonesian satay, but I have turned it into a tasty, saucy stir-fry using seitan (although you could also try it with smoked tofu). Serving it on courgette noodles gives the whole dish a fresher, lighter twist.

250g (9oz) seitan pieces, drained

½ tsp ground turmeric

½ tsp ground coriander

1 lemongrass stalk, finely grated

pinch of sea salt

pinch of ground white pepper

1 tbsp cornflour

1 tbsp rapeseed oil

1 tbsp Shaohsing rice wine or dry sherry

1–2 tbsp tamari or low-sodium light soy sauce

2 courgettes, spiralised

For the satay sauce

1 garlic clove, roughly chopped

1 red chilli, deseeded and roughly chopped

1 large shallot, roughly chopped

½ tsp tamarind paste

1 tsp sriracha

3 tbsp crunchy peanut butter

1 tbsp golden syrup

150ml (5fl oz) coconut milk (see tip on page 67)

50ml (2fl oz) hot water

To serve

handful of raw beansprouts, washed

freshly chopped coriander leaves

1 spring onion, trimmed and sliced on the angle

lime wedges and freshly sliced red chillies

Place the seitan in a shallow bowl and add the turmeric, ground coriander, lemongrass, sea salt and white pepper, stirring to evenly season the seitan. Dust the seasoned seitan with cornflour and set aside.

Place all the ingredients for the satay sauce in a food processor. Blitz well to create a smooth sauce and set aside until needed.

Heat a wok over a high heat. When it starts to smoke, add the rapeseed oil. Once hot, add the seitan pieces and cook, tossing, for a few seconds to sear on all sides.

Season with the rice wine or sherry and tamari or light soy sauce, then pour in the satay sauce and bring to the boil. Reduce the heat and simmer for 8–10 minutes until it has thickened and is a rich brown colour.

The courgette noodles can be used raw, or if you prefer, you can poach them lightly in hot water before dividing them between two plates. Spoon the satay seitan over the top. Garnish with the beansprouts, coriander, spring onion, lime wedges and fresh chillies and serve immediately.

6.   Sharing Plates

Golden Sticky Rice Cabbage 'Money Bag' Parcels

kcal — 269
carbs — 46.3g
protein — 8.3g
fat — 6.4g

Makes 6 parcels

15 min   20 min

The trick to a good sticky fried rice is to stir through some toasted sesame oil to help separate the grains in the wok. The cabbage leaves need to be blanched until they are soft, but not so soft that they break. You can leave these parcels open or use chives to tie them closed. The dish holds well in a steamer, too: just reheat before you serve.

300g (10½oz) glutinous rice, washed until the water runs clear

300ml (10fl oz) vegetable stock

1 tbsp + 1 tsp toasted sesame oil

1 tbsp rapeseed oil

1 garlic clove, finely chopped

1 tsp finely grated fresh root ginger

1 red chilli, deseeded and finely chopped

1 small carrot, finely diced

¼ tsp ground turmeric

100g (3½oz) smoked tofu, drained, rinsed in cold water and diced into 3mm (⅛in) cubes

50g (1¾oz) long-stem broccoli, finely diced

6 fresh shiitake mushrooms, stems discarded, sliced

2–3 tbsp tamari or low-sodium light soy sauce

1 tbsp brown rice vinegar

1 spring onion, trimmed and finely chopped

small handful of coriander, finely chopped

For the 'money bag' parcels

6 whole savoy cabbage leaves

6 garlic chives or onion chives

To garnish

micro shiso

micro coriander

edible flowers

Put the rice in a saucepan over a medium heat. Add the stock and bring to the boil, then cover with a lid, reduce the heat and simmer for 15 minutes until all the stock has been absorbed.

Turn the rice out on to a tray and cool at room temperature for 15 minutes. Once cool, add 1 tbsp sesame oil to stop the rice from sticking together when it's added to the wok.

Meanwhile, prepare the cabbage leaves. Prepare a saucepan of hot water and a bowl of iced water. Blanch the cabbage leaves in the hot water until tender (less than a minute), then rinse, drain, plunge into the iced water and pat dry with kitchen paper. Set aside.

Place a wok over a high heat until smoking, and add the rapeseed oil. Once hot, add the garlic, ginger and chilli and stir-fry for 3 seconds, then add the carrot and turmeric and cook, tossing, for 10 seconds.

Add the tofu, broccoli and mushrooms and toss for a further 10 seconds. Now add the rice and start to break it down, but don't stab at it and make it claggy. Season with the tamari or light soy sauce and rice vinegar, pouring them evenly across the rice, followed by 1 tsp toasted sesame oil. Stir-fry for 2 minutes to mix the flavours. The rice should be quite 'clean' and golden in colour. Sprinkle over the spring onion and coriander.

To create the 'money bags', spoon some of the rice mixture into one of the cabbage leaves. Use a chive to tie it into a money bag shape. Repeat with the remaining cabbage leaves and rice, garnish with the micro herbs and flowers and serve immediately.

Sweet & Spicy Chilli Bean Tofu, Water Chestnut & Spring Onion Skewers

kcal — 203
carbs — 19.0g
protein — 7.5g
fat — 11.0g

Makes 6–8 skewers

20 min   7 min

These are perfect for a light supper or can be scaled up for barbecues during the summer months. Extra firm tofu is marinated in a sweet and spicy chilli bean sauce and then skewered alongside sweet, nutty water chestnuts and spring onions, and cooked until slightly sticky-sweet. Serve with a crunchy noodle salad topped with cashews. So good!
You will need 6–8 bamboo skewers, pre-soaked in cold water.

400g (14oz) extra firm tofu, drained, and sliced into rectangular blocks of about 1.5 x 3cm (¾ x 1¼in)

225g (8oz) can whole water chestnuts, drained

3 spring onions, trimmed and sliced into 2.5cm (1in) pieces

1 tbsp rapeseed oil, plus extra for drizzling

For the marinade

1 tbsp freshly grated root ginger

1 tbsp chilli bean sauce

1 tbsp dark soy sauce

2 tbsp golden syrup

1 tbsp clear rice vinegar

1 tbsp toasted sesame oil

For the salad

100g (3½oz) vermicelli rice noodles

1 tbsp sesame oil

2 Chinese leaves, shredded

1 large carrot, sliced into julienne strips

100g (3½oz) radishes, sliced into julienne strips

2 spring onions, trimmed and finely sliced

handful of roasted salted cashew nuts

For the salad dressing

2 tbsp tamari or low-sodium light soy sauce

1 tbsp toasted sesame oil

1 tbsp olive oil

juice of 1 lime

Place all the marinade ingredients in a jar. Put the lid on and shake well to combine. Place the tofu pieces in a non-metallic bowl and pour the marinade over, combining to mix well. Transfer to the refrigerator for 20 minutes to marinate.

Meanwhile, cook the vermicelli rice noodles for the salad for 3 minutes. Drain and dress with the sesame oil, then set aside until needed.

Combine the salad dressing ingredients in a jar and shake well to mix. Set aside until needed.

In a salad bowl, combine the shredded Chinese leaves, carrot, radishes, noodles and spring onions. Cover and place in the refrigerator to chill.

Prepare the skewers. First thread on a piece of marinated tofu (lengthways), following by a water chestnut, then a piece of spring onion. Repeat this pattern about three times for each skewer.

Heat a griddle pan over a medium heat. Just before cooking, brush the rapeseed oil over the griddle, and also drizzle some over the skewers (this will help them cook and prevent them from sticking to the griddle).

Carefully lay each skewer on the griddle and cook for 1½ minutes on each side, until you can easily lift the tofu off the griddle. (Do take care when doing so to prevent it from breaking.)

Once cooked, lay the skewers on a serving plate. Pour the dressing over the salad, add the cashew nuts, and toss to mix well. Serve the noodle salad alongside the tofu skewers and eat immediately.

Edamame
& Avocado Toast

5 min

Serves 1–2
(makes 2
slices)

kcal — 333
carbs — 28.3g
protein — 12.5g
fat — 18.0g

Wasabi, Water Chestnut
& Spring Onion Dip

5 min

Serves 2

kcal — 137
carbs — 15.7g
protein — 3.9g
fat — 7.1g

If you are using frozen edamame beans, give them a quick blanch in boiling water, then drain and refresh in cold water. You can add slices of smoked tofu or grilled long-stem broccoli to turn this into a light supper.

2 slices of plain sourdough bread, toasted

For the edamame & avocado mash

100g (3½oz) edamame beans, boiled, drained and cooled

1 red chilli

1 avocado, peeled and stoned

juice of ½ lemon

1 spring onion, trimmed and sliced

small handful of coriander

pinch of sea salt

pinch of freshly ground black pepper

To garnish

shichimi togarashi pepper flakes

tamari or low-sodium light soy sauce

Place all the ingredients for the edamame and avocado mash in a food processor and blitz.

Spoon the mash over the sourdough toast. Sprinkle over some shichimi togarashi pepper flakes, drizzle on some tamari or light soy sauce, and eat immediately.

Not only are water chestnuts delicious in stir-fries or curries, they also make a healthy, light, super easy dip. Their sweet, nutty flavour is gorgeous when seasoned with wasabi, tamari and white pepper.

For the dip

225g (8oz) can water chestnuts

1 tbsp sesame oil

1 spring onion, trimmed and roughly chopped

2 tsp wasabi paste

1 tbsp tamari or low-sodium light soy sauce

large pinch of ground white pepper

To serve

½ cucumber, sliced into batons

1 carrot, sliced into batons

2 celery sticks, sliced into batons

a handful of cauliflower florets

a handful of cherry tomatoes

OR

oven-baked pitta bread

Place all the dip ingredients in a food processor and blend to combine.

Spoon out into a small bowl. Serve with your favourite crudités or oven-baked pitta bread.

Sharing Plates

Korean Mushroom Barbecue 'Tapas'

kcal — 387
carbs — 69.5g
protein — 8.8g
fat — 9.9g

Serves 4 to share

25 min   25 min

I really enjoy Korean food for its strong, punchy flavours, achieved using garlic and spice pastes such as doenjang. This is one of my favourite dishes to cook and eat, and it was taught to me by my vegan friend Ellie Koon. Thank you, Ellie, for the inspiration. It is the perfect dish for everyone to get involved and make their own Korean barbecue wraps.

300g (10½oz) jasmine rice

1 daikon, peeled and sliced using a mandolin into thin 7–8cm rounds

1 tbsp clear rice vinegar or seasoned sushi vinegar

12 perilla leaves and 2 little gem lettuce heads to give approx. 20 leaves in total (double the quantity of gem lettuce if you can't get perilla)

1–2 tbsp toasted sesame oil

4 x 5g (⅛oz) packs thin crispy fried seaweed, shredded in a food processor

ssamjang, to serve

doenjang, to serve

For the wok-fried mushrooms

1 tbsp rapeseed oil

large pinch of sea salt

large pinch of golden caster sugar

6 garlic cloves, peeled and left whole

200g (7oz) enoki mushrooms

200g (7oz) fresh shiitake mushrooms, sliced

1 tbsp Shaohsing rice wine or dry sherry

1 tbsp tamari or low-sodium light soy sauce

large pinch of freshly ground black pepper

1 tbsp toasted sesame oil

Wash the rice well until the water runs clear. Place the rice in a medium-sized saucepan over a medium heat. Add 600ml (20fl oz) water and bring to the boil. Reduce the heat to low, cover the pan with a tight-fitting lid, and let the rice cook in its own steam for 20 minutes. When the rice is cooked, fluff up the grains and pour into a shallow dish to cool. Leave to stand for 30 minutes.

Meanwhile, place the daikon in a container and drizzle over the rice vinegar or sushi vinegar. Set aside in the refrigerator to 'pickle'. Prepare the perilla or lettuce leaves. Separate the leaves, wash and pat dry, then place on damp kitchen towels to keep fresh. Chill in the refrigerator until you are ready to serve.

Once the rice is cooled, drizzle over some toasted sesame oil. Sprinkle over the fried crispy seaweed flakes. With clean hands, take a tablespoon of the rice and roll it in the palms of your hands to make a small, oval ball – it should come to a slight point at the ends. Keep going to make 20 crispy seaweed hand-rolled rice balls. Set aside.

Heat a wok over a high heat until smoking and add the rapeseed oil. Once hot, add the salt, sugar and garlic, followed by the mushrooms. Cook, stirring, for 2–3 minutes until the mushrooms are wilted and slightly browned at the edges. Stir through the rice wine or sherry, tamari or light soy sauce, black pepper and toasted sesame oil. Spoon out onto a serving plate.

To serve, lay out all the components on the table, including ssamjang or doenjang in little bowls. To assemble, take a perilla or little gem leaf in your palm and layer with daikon. Place a small ball of seaweed rice in the centre, top with mushrooms and a garlic clove, and finish with a dollop of ssamjang or doenjang. Wrap up the leaf and eat immediately.

Edamame & Shiitake Inari Rice Pockets

kcal — 403
carbs — 61.3g
protein — 13.2g
fat — 12.1g

Serves 2–4 to share
(makes 12–14 pockets)

25 min   1–2 min

Inari bean curd pockets are easily found in the frozen sections of Japanese supermarkets – all you have to do is to defrost them. If you can't find them, use little gem or iceberg lettuce leaves instead. Served with a simple dipping sauce of soy sauce, rice vinegar and sesame oil, these make a great appetiser when you're entertaining, but can also be enjoyed as a healthy light supper or snack. They're also great for a packed lunch or a picnic.

12–14 dried shiitake mushroom strips

1 tbsp rapeseed oil

2.5cm (1in) piece of fresh root ginger, finely grated

1 tbsp mirin

1 tbsp tamari or low-sodium light soy sauce

1 tsp dark soy sauce

1 tbsp rice vinegar

12–14 inari pockets (or lettuce leaves – see above)

For the rice

100g (3½oz) sushi rice

100g (3½oz) wild rice

1 tsp vegetable bouillon powder

1 tbsp rice vinegar

1 tbsp mirin

pinch of golden caster sugar

100g (3½oz) frozen edamame beans, defrosted

2 tbsp black sesame seeds

To serve

shichimi togarashi pepper flakes

pickled ginger

Begin by preparing the rice. Wash the sushi rice and wild rice well and rinse until the water runs clear. Place in a medium-sized saucepan over a medium heat and add 400ml (14fl oz) water. Add the vegetable bouillon powder and stir well to dissolve. Bring to the boil, then cover with a tight-fitting lid. Reduce the heat to very low and cook for 15–20 minutes. Remove the lid and fluff up the grains with a fork, then spoon out the rice on to a tray to cool.

While the rice is still warm, mix together the rice vinegar, mirin and sugar in a bowl. Stir well to dissolve, then pour this sweet dressing over the rice. Set aside. Meanwhile, soak the dried mushrooms for 10 minutes in boiling water, then drain.

Heat a wok over a high heat until smoking, and add the rapeseed oil. Once hot, add the ginger and cook, stirring, for a few seconds. Then add the drained mushrooms and stir-fry for a few seconds more. Stir in the mirin, tamari or light soy sauce, dark soy sauce and rice vinegar and cook for 1–2 minutes until the mushrooms are caramelised at the edges. Set aside on a plate to cool.

Sprinkle the edamame beans and black sesame seeds over the rice and stir to combine.

To assemble, take one of the inari pockets and place a layer of the seasoned mushroom mixture around the edge of the pocket. Fill the rest with the mixed edamame and sesame seed rice mixture. Repeat with the remaining pockets and fillings.

Sprinkle some shichimi togarashi pepper flakes over the top of each one, plus more on the side of the plate for dipping into. Serve with pickled ginger on the side.

Sharing Plates

Vietnamese Mushroom & Asparagus Raw Spring Rolls

kcal — 270
carbs — 39.7g
protein — 9.0g
fat — 9.2g

Serves 2–4 to share
(makes 8 spring rolls)

25 min   2–3 min

I love these raw, open spring roll-style wraps. They are super easy to make and extremely delicious! The trick is to marinate and grill the mushrooms first, then wrap them with your favourite salad ingredients and some smoked tofu. Don't be put off by the long list of ingredients: we're also making a simple dipping sauce, and many of the ingredients are raw. Hope you love these as much as I do.

For the asparagus & mushrooms

3–4 tbsp Vietnamese soy sauce, tamari or low-sodium light soy sauce

1 tbsp mirin

1 lemongrass stalk, grated

2 tbsp golden syrup

2 garlic cloves, finely chopped

4 asparagus spears, hard end of stalk snapped off, sliced in half on the angle

8 whole oyster mushrooms

1 tbsp rapeseed oil

For the sesame seed dipping sauce

2 tbsp toasted white sesame seeds

1 red chilli, roughly sliced (retain seeds if you want it spicy, otherwise remove)

1 tbsp Vietnamese soy sauce, tamari or low-sodium light soy sauce

2–3 tbsp golden caster sugar

1 tsp toasted sesame oil

small handful of freshly chopped coriander

juice of 1 lime

To assemble

8 Vietnamese rice paper wrappers

3 romaine lettuce leaves, stalks removed

6 spring onions, green parts only, sliced into 10cm (4in) julienne strips

1 carrot, sliced into julienne strips

100g (3½oz) smoked tofu, drained, rinsed in cold water, grilled and sliced into julienne strips

a few sprigs of Vietnamese mint

Begin by making a marinade for the asparagus, mushrooms and smoked tofu. In a bowl, combine the Vietnamese soy sauce, tamari or light soy sauce and mirin. Add the grated lemongrass, golden syrup and garlic and stir to combine well.

Toss the asparagus and mushrooms in the marinade to lightly coat. Drizzle over the rapeseed oil. Remove the vegetables from the marinade and set aside on a plate. Retain the rest of the marinade for basting.

Heat a griddle pan over a medium heat. Add the asparagus pieces and mushrooms and grill for 2–3 minutes, turning the vegetables regularly and using a brush to baste them with the remaining marinade liquid. Set aside.

Now make the sesame seed dipping sauce. In a pestle and mortar, crush the sesame seeds. Add the chilli, Vietnamese soy sauce, tamari or light soy sauce, sugar, toasted sesame oil and coriander. Squeeze in some lime juice and mix well.

When you're ready to assemble, lay out all the ingredients on your work surface.

Dip the rice paper wrappers in hot water until pliable. Lay out a rice paper wrapper and fill it first with romaine lettuce, then oyster mushrooms and asparagus, then spring onion and carrot strips. Finally, top with the smoked tofu strips and layer on some mint leaves.

Working quickly, wrap the rice paper wrapper over the vegetables to form a cone or a 'hand roll' shape, leaving one end open like a bouquet. Repeat with the remaining rolls and fillings.

Serve with the sesame seed dipping sauce.

Spicy Korean Courgette & Tofu Stew

kcal — 171
carbs — 10.0g
protein — 8.9g
fat — 10.5g

Serves 4

25 min   10 min

This is an addictive, spicy tofu stew taught to me by the incredible Korean chef, Judy Joo. Traditionally the recipe calls for silken tofu, but I'm using firm tofu here – use whichever you prefer. You can add whatever vegetables you have in the refrigerator: corn on the cob, daikon, seasonal greens, broccoli, edamame… You can make it even quicker if you use ready-made vegetable stock instead of making your own.

1 tbsp rapeseed oil

½ onion, diced

2 garlic cloves, crushed and finely chopped

2.5cm (1in) piece of fresh root ginger, grated

2 tbsp gochugaru (Korean red chilli flakes)

1 large handful of Chinese leaf, sliced into 2.5cm (1in) strips

1 courgette, sliced lengthways and then sliced into 5mm (¼in) slices

large handful of assorted Asian mushrooms

200g (7oz) fresh firm tofu, drained, and sliced into 1.5cm (¾in) chunks

large handful of baby spinach leaves

sea salt, to taste

For the stock

1.2 litres (2 pints) water

small handful of sliced dried shiitake mushrooms

1 tbsp vegetable bouillon powder

½ onion, sliced

2.5cm (1in) piece of dried kelp (optional)

To serve

toasted sesame oil

roasted white sesame seeds

small handful of onion chives, freshly chopped

cooked jasmine rice, to serve (optional, see page 194)

Place a large stockpot over a medium heat. Add all the stock ingredients and bring to a simmer for 20 minutes. Alternatively, just use 1.2 litres (2 pints) of water or ready-made vegetable stock.

When the stock is ready, heat a wok over a medium heat until slightly smoking, then add the rapeseed oil. Once hot, add the onion and stir-fry for 2 minutes, until softened and translucent. Add the garlic, ginger and gochugaru and cook, stirring, for a few seconds. Then add the Chinese leaf and courgette, along with the stock, and bring to the boil.

Reduce the heat and simmer for 4 minutes until the Chinese leaf has softened and the courgettes are yellow-green but not overcooked, and still have a bite.

Add the mushrooms and tofu and cook for a further 3 minutes, being careful not to break up the tofu. Add the spinach, season to taste with sea salt and stir well.

Take the stew off the heat and divide between four bowls. Garnish the stew with a drizzle of toasted sesame oil and a scattering of roasted white sesame seeds and onion chives. Eat immediately, with a bowl of plain jasmine rice on the side, if you like.

Fragrant Lemongrass Tofu & Chickpea Balls with Sweet Chilli Sauce

kcal — 152
carbs — 17.5g
protein — 5.6g
fat — 7.0g

Serves 6 to share
(makes 30 balls)

15 min

5–8 min
cooking
in batches

Tofu and chickpeas are my new best friends. When partnered with aromatic herbs like ginger, lemongrass and coriander, these humble ingredients transform into something amazing. This is a simple, tasty appetiser, perfect for a big party. You can even fry the balls in advance and keep them hot in the oven until ready to serve and assemble.

200g (7oz) fresh firm tofu, drained and roughly chopped

1 tbsp freshly grated root ginger

1 lemongrass stalk, finely grated

pinch of sea salt

pinch of finely ground white pepper

1 tbsp cornflour

3 tbsp aquafaba (taken from the canned chickpeas below)

100g (3½oz) canned chickpeas

1 red chilli, deseeded and finely chopped

1 small handful of coriander stalks, finely chopped

1 spring onion, trimmed and finely chopped

50g (1¾oz) plain flour

500ml (18fl oz) vegetable oil

To serve

50g (1¾oz) baby spinach leaves, washed, drained

1 tbsp shichimi togarashi pepper flakes

50ml (2fl oz) sweet chilli sauce

Place the tofu, ginger, lemongrass, salt and white pepper in a food processor and blitz to a smooth consistency.

In a small bowl, mix together the cornflour and aquafaba using a fork until well combined. Pour this mixture into the food processor and blitz to combine.

Transfer the tofu mixture from the food processer into a bowl.

Place the chickpeas in the food processor and pulse until you have small pieces. Alternatively, you can use a knife to roughly chop them. You want the pieces to be a bit coarse and chunky. Stir the chickpeas into the tofu mixture.

Add the chilli, coriander stalks and spring onion to the mixture and mix to combine well.

Using wetted hands, form the mixture into about 30 small balls. Dust the balls with the plain flour and set aside.

Heat a wok over a high heat until smoking and pour in the vegetable oil. Working in batches, use a metal spider strainer or slotted spoon to gently lower the balls into the oil, spooning some oil over them to brown them all over. Fry the balls for 2–3 minutes until golden brown. Carefully remove from the wok and place on a heatproof plate lined with kitchen paper to drain well. Repeat with the remaining balls.

To serve, place each ball on a spinach leaf, sprinkle over some shichimi togarashi pepper flakes and drizzle with a small dollop of sweet chilli sauce. Serve immediately.

Sharing Plates

Sweet Chilli 'Shawarma' Burger

kcal — 651
carbs — 60.7g
protein —47.7g
fat — 23.5g

Serves 2

15 min   3–4 min

This is a fusion mix of two of my favourite cuisines – Lebanese and American-Chinese. My best friend of 30 years, Lina, used to invite me to her house every Saturday night for a Lebanese dinner. So, when we wanted a plant-based option, we made a shawarma-spiced seitan. Together with an Asian-inspired slaw, this dish was born! For best results, pre-slice and chill the slaw ingredients in the refrigerator so that, when you come to assemble them, the slaw is nice and cold.

1 tbsp rapeseed oil

1 garlic cloves, finely chopped

2.5cm (1in) piece of fresh root ginger, finely grated

1 tsp dark soy sauce

1 tbsp sweet chilli sauce

1 tbsp Shaohsing rice wine or dry sherry

2 vegan brioche buns or seeded wholemeal buns

2 tbsp hoisin sauce

2 tbsp vegan mayonnaise

1 tsp sriracha

For the shawarma-spiced seitan

¼ tsp freshly ground black pepper

¼ tsp ground all spice

¼ tsp garlic or onion powder, or vegetable bouillon powder

pinch of ground cloves

pinch of ground nutmeg

pinch of ground cardamom

2 pinches of dried chilli flakes

pinch of dried oregano

pinch of cracked sea salt

330g (11¾oz) seitan pieces, drained and sliced

For the sesame slaw

1 tbsp tahini

1 tsp maple or agave syrup

2 tbsp tamari or low-sodium light soy sauce

1 tsp toasted sesame oil

1 tbsp brown rice vinegar

2 carrots, sliced into fine julienne strips

100g (3½oz) red cabbage, sliced into fine julienne strips

100g (3½oz) white cabbage, sliced into fine julienne strips

½ red onion, sliced into fine julienne strips

1 spring onion, trimmed and finely chopped

juice of ½ lime

1 small handful of chives, chopped

Begin by making the slaw. Mix together the tahini, maple or agave syrup, tamari or light soy sauce, toasted sesame oil and brown rice vinegar in a jar. Shake to combine.

In a large salad bowl, combine the carrots, red and white cabbage, red onion and spring onion. Pour over the slaw dressing. Squeeze over some lime juice and garnish with chives. Set aside.

Now prepare the shawarma-spiced seitan. In a small bowl, mix together the spices. Lay the seitan pieces out on a plate and evenly sprinkle the spice mix over them. Set aside until needed.

Heat a wok over a high heat until smoking. Add the rapeseed oil and give the wok a swirl. Once hot, add the garlic and ginger and toss for a few seconds. Add the sharwarma-spiced seitan pieces and cook, stirring,

for 20 seconds. Stir in the dark soy and sweet chilli sauces, and deglaze with the rice wine or sherry. Mix well and transfer the contents of the wok to a heatproof plate.

Slice the buns in half and place them cut-side down on the wok for 20 seconds to toast. Remove from the wok and slather a layer of hoisin sauce on the insides of each bun.

In a small bowl, mix together the vegan mayo and sriracha to make a vegan sriracha mayo.

Spoon some sticky shawarma pieces on to the base of a bun. Top with some slaw, then add another layer of shawarma, and top with more slaw. Drizzle over some sriracha may and top with the other half of the bun. Repeat for the other burger and serve.

Peking Mushroom Pancakes

kcal — 268
carbs — 34.8g
protein — 6.4g
fat — 11.4g

Serves 4 to share

10 min

10–12 min

These are an easy and tasty alternative to Peking duck pancakes. Instead of duck, I have used an array of mushrooms. If you are not a fan of mushrooms, you can use seitan, smoked tofu, cauliflower or courgettes, but the mushrooms really do work well – they provide a bold umami flavour and take on the Chinese five spice brilliantly.

500g (1lb 2oz) mixed mushrooms – I used shiitake, oyster, king trumpet and shimeji mushrooms

1 tbsp Chinese five spice

large pinch of dried chilli flakes

pinch of sea salt

1 tbsp tamari or low-sodium light soy sauce

3 tbsp rapeseed oil

To serve

16–18 shop-bought wheat-flour pancakes (or use washed little gem lettuce leaves)

5 tbsp hoisin sauce

2 spring onions, trimmed and sliced into julienne strips

1 cucumber, deseeded and sliced into julienne strips

Preheat the oven to 180°C/160°C fan/350°F/Gas Mark 4.

Place all the mushrooms on a roasting tray. Sprinkle over the Chinese five spice, chilli flakes and sea salt, and drizzle over the tamari or light soy sauce and rapeseed oil. Roast in the oven for 10–12 minutes.

Meanwhile, place the pancakes in a small bamboo steamer set up over a wok half-filled with water. Steam the pancakes for 8 minutes, then take off the heat and set aside.

To serve, transfer the mushrooms to a serving plate, and place the hoisin sauce, spring onions and cucumber in small, individual dishes. Place the steamer basket of pancakes on the table and let everyone help themselves.

Asian-style Hot Dogs

kcal — 370
carbs — 53.4g
protein — 17.7g
fat — 10.2g

Serves 6

15 min

15–20 min

Hot dogs instantly take me to sunny days and barbecues outdoors. I love this recipe: the umami-rich, sticky onion and tomatoes, combined with the spicy corn and tart mustard, give layers of flavour. These tasty toppings elevate shop-bought vegan sausages to the next level. To me, it's the perfect hot dog. You can scale up the quantities to make a hot dog stand for barbecues and parties. It's so easy and delicious to make.

6 vegan sausages (I use Linda McCartney sausages)

6 plain hot dog rolls

1 tsp olive oil spread

handful of baby spinach leaves

2 tbsp mustard of your choice (I use French's mustard)

For the onion & tomato relish

1 tbsp rapeseed oil

2 red onions, sliced

5 cherry tomatoes, halved

pinch of dried chilli flakes

1 tbsp tamari or low-sodium light soy sauce

2 tbsp golden syrup

For the spicy sweetcorn

1 tbsp rapeseed oil

1 spring onion, trimmed and finely sliced

340g (12oz) can sweetcorn, drained

1 tsp sriracha

1 tbsp tamari or low-sodium light soy sauce

Cook the sausages according to the packet instructions.

Meanwhile, to make the onion and tomato relish, heat a wok over a medium heat. Add the rapeseed oil and give the oil a swirl. Add the red onions and cherry tomatoes and cook, stirring, for 30 seconds. Stir in the dried chilli flakes, tamari or light soy sauce and golden syrup and cook for another 2–3 minutes until softened. Transfer to a heatproof bowl and set aside.

Now make the spicy sweetcorn. Wash and wipe out the wok and reheat. Add the rapeseed oil and give the oil a swirl, then add the spring onion and stir-fry for a few seconds. Add the sweetcorn, sriracha and tamari or light soy sauce and stir-fry for 1 minute until combined well. Set aside until needed.

Heat a griddle pan over a medium heat until slightly smoking. Slice open the hot dog rolls and spread with olive oil spread. Place on the griddle pan spread side down for 20 seconds, then remove. Some of the rolls may break in half but try to keep them intact.

To assemble the hot dogs, place some spinach leaves in the hot dog rolls, followed by the cooked vegan sausages. Spoon over the spicy sweetcorn, dress with sticky onion and tomato relish and squeeze over some mustard. Serve and eat immediately.

Fragrant Minced Soy Stuffed Aubergines

kcal — 317
carbs — 13.3g
protein — 13.4g
fat — 23.7g

Serves 2 or 4 to share (makes 12 stuffed aubergines)

15 min   10 min

This dish is inspired by Sichuan fragrant aubergines. I decided to turn baby aubergines into a dim sum bite-sized 'boat'. Grilling the aubergines first helps makes them softer, and also means you can shallow-fry them to cook the filling rather than deep-frying. The result is an excellent 'veggie-meaty' dish.

110g (3¾oz) dehydrated minced soy

200ml (7fl oz) boiling water or vegetable stock

6 baby aubergines, halved

pinch of sea salt flakes

pinch of ground white pepper

1 tbsp rapeseed oil

rapeseed oil or sunflower oil, for frying

For the filling

pinch of sea salt flakes

pinch of ground white pepper

1 tbsp freshly grated root ginger

50ml (2fl oz) aquafaba

1 tbsp vegetarian mushroom sauce

1 tsp toasted sesame oil

1 spring onion, trimmed and finely chopped

2 tbsp cornflour

To serve

1 tbsp finely chopped chives

toasted white sesame seeds

2.5cm (1in) piece of fresh root ginger, sliced into matchsticks

1–2 tbsp Chinkiang black rice vinegar

To rehydrate the minced soy, add the hot water or stock and leave to stand for 5 minutes. Season the halved aubergines with sea salt and ground white pepper and drizzle over 1 tbsp rapeseed oil.

Heat a griddle pan over a high heat until smoking. Once hot, place the aubergines in the pan, flesh-side down, and cook for 1–2 minutes. Flip over to cook on the other side for another 1–2 minutes until soft. Remove from the pan and set aside.

Place all the filling ingredients in a food processor. Blitz to create a chunky paste – you don't want it too smooth. Set aside.

To prepare the aubergine halves for stuffing, slice down the soft centre of each one, cutting about halfway through, not completely. Take a small teaspoon of the filling and fill the inside of each aubergine half using the slits you have just created, so that the mound is about 1cm (½in) high on top of each aubergine half.

Heat a frying pan over a medium heat and pour in enough rapeseed oil or sunflower oil to fill the pan to a depth of about 2.5cm (1in). Heat the oil to 180°C (350°F), or until a cube of bread turns golden-brown in 15 seconds and floats to the surface. Working in batches, gently place the aubergine pieces, filling side-down, into the oil and fry for about 2 minutes until the fragrant soy filling is cooked through. Transfer to a plate lined with kitchen paper to drain.

To serve, place the aubergine halves on a plate and sprinkle over some finely chopped chives and toasted white sesame seeds. Mix the ginger matchsticks and black rice vinegar together in a small bowl and serve alongside the aubergines.

Chinese Black Bean Seitan Tacos

kcal — 633
carbs — 45.4g
protein — 30.4g
fat — 35.7g

Serves 2

15 min   5 min

Black bean sauce is packed full of savoury umami and pairs perfectly with crunchy peppers. This combination is traditionally used in a classic Cantonese dish, but I'm turning it into a delicious filling for some Mexican tacos. The black bean filling contrasts with the creamy avocado, bright pickles and fresh chilli, making this a flavour-packed fusion dish.

1 tbsp rapeseed oil

2 garlic cloves, finely chopped

1 red chilli, deseeded and finely chopped

1 large onion, sliced into half-moon slices

200g (7oz) seitan, drained and sliced into strips

1 tbsp shop-bought black bean and garlic sauce

1 green pepper, finely sliced

1 tbsp tamari or low-sodium light soy sauce

For the quick-pickled onions

1 red onion, finely sliced

2 tbsp apple cider vinegar

For the sriracha mayonnaise

1 tbsp sriracha

2 tbsp shop-bought vegan mayonnaise

To serve

4 wheat-flour tacos

1 avocado, peeled, stoned and mashed

100g (3½oz) pink radishes, finely sliced

1 red chilli, deseeded and finely chopped

coriander leaves, to garnish

Begin by getting all the 'serve with' items ready. For the quick-pickled onions, mix together the red onion and the apple cider vinegar in a small bowl and set aside. For the sriracha mayonnaise, simply mix together the sriracha and mayonnaise in a small bowl. Arrange the mashed avocado, sliced radishes, chopped chilli and coriander leaves in small bowls, ready to go.

To prepare the tacos, place a flat-bottomed pan over a low–medium heat and heat the tacos one at a time to warm through. Transfer to a warmed plate and cover with foil. Keep them warm in a low oven until you are ready to serve.

Now heat a wok over a medium heat and add the rapeseed oil. Once hot, add the garlic and chilli and stir-fry for a few seconds, then add the onion and cook for 1 minute until translucent, with a smoky char at the edges. Add the seitan strips, followed by the black bean and garlic sauce. Toss together well. Next add the green peppers and cook, tossing, for less than 1 minute.

Season with tamari or light soy sauce and continue to cook, stirring all the time, for 1 minute until the flavours have coated the seitan well. You want the peppers to be crisp, with a slight sear on the edges. Remove from the heat and transfer the contents of the wok to a serving plate.

Transfer all the taco components to the table to serve. To assemble a taco, place some of the black bean seitan in the centre, followed by some creamy avocado and pink radish slices. Drizzle over some vegan sriracha mayo, and garnish with fresh chillies, pickled red onions and fresh coriander leaves.

7. Sweet
Tooth

Banana & Chocolate Ice Cream with Mango

Serves 1

kcal — 357
carbs — 70.8g
protein — 7.7g
fat — 6.8g

5 min

This is an easy dessert that is healthy and delish, and a great way to use up any overripe bananas in your fruit bowl. The only downside? You have to eat it quick before it melts! You can mix it up and use your favourite fruits and toppings.

3 frozen bananas

3 tbsp cocoa powder

1 tbsp chocolate almond milk

To serve

finely diced mango

dark chocolate cacao nibs

1 Oreo™ thin

Place the frozen bananas, cocoa powder and chocolate almond milk in a blender. Blend until smooth.

Transfer to a bowl and garnish with mango, cacao nibs and the Oreo™ thin. Serve immediately.

Roasted Star Anise Pineapple

Serves 4

kcal — 204
carbs — 29.5g
protein — 2.9g
fat — 8.8g

15 min   35 min

This simple, fragrant roasted pineapple in a sweet orange syrup is delightful served warm with a creamy, light, lime-zesty coconut yogurt, topped with toasted cashew nuts. An easy, healthy, straightforward recipe, perfect all year round.

1 large pineapple, peeled, cored and sliced into wedge-shaped pieces

zest and juice of 2 oranges

3 tbsp golden syrup

2 star anise

2.5cm (1in) piece of fresh root ginger, grated

1 tsp vanilla extract

To serve

200g (7oz) coconut yogurt

1 tbsp golden syrup

zest and juice of 1 lime

small handful of crushed roasted salted cashews

Preheat the oven to 180°C/160°C fan/350°F/Gas Mark 4.

Place the pineapple wedges in a baking dish and add the orange zest and juice, golden syrup, star anise, ginger and vanilla extract. Toss to coat well. Cover with kitchen foil and roast in the oven for 35 minutes.

Meanwhile, mix together the coconut yogurt, golden syrup and lime zest and juice and set aside until needed. Remove the roasted pineapple from the oven and divide between four bowls.

Top each bowl with a dollop of the flavoured coconut yogurt and sprinkle over some roasted chopped cashews. Serve immediately.

Sweet Tooth

Pineapple
& Walnut Loaf

kcal — 380
carbs — 36.5g
protein — 6.9g
fat — 23.3g

Serves 8

10 min

35–40 min

I love banana loaf, but here I decided to use pineapples instead. The result is a subtle, sweet, nutty loaf, perfect with a cup of green tea. To keep this light and healthy, I haven't added much sugar. If you prefer a sweeter taste, drizzle over some golden syrup.

olive oil spread, for greasing

4 canned pineapple rings (see tip)

60g (2¼oz) ground almonds

185g (6½oz) gluten-free plain flour

2 tsp gluten-free baking powder

1 tsp ground cinnamon

100g (3½oz) golden caster sugar

¼ tsp sea salt

125ml (4fl oz) coconut milk

75ml (2½fl oz) rapeseed oil

1 tsp vanilla extract

50g (1¾oz) crushed walnut pieces

coconut dairy-free ice cream, to garnish

zest and juice of 1 lime, to garnish

Preheat the oven to 180°C/160°C fan/350°F/Gas Mark 4. Grease and line a 900g (2lb) loaf tin with baking paper.

Drain the pineapple and blitz in a food processor to create a purée. Set aside.

Sift the ground almonds and flour into a mixing bowl and add the baking powder, cinnamon, sugar and sea salt. Mix well to combine.

Add the coconut milk, rapeseed oil, vanilla extract and pineapple purée. Mix well to form a smooth batter. Sprinkle in the walnut pieces.

Pour the batter into the prepared tin and bake for 35–40 minutes until the cake is golden and a skewer inserted into the middle comes out clean.

Transfer to a wire rack and leave to cool for 5 minutes, then slice.

Serve warm, with coconut ice cream. Sprinkle over the lime zest and juice and eat immediately.

Ching's Tip — Keep the juice from the pineapple can to use in a sweet and sour dish.

Golden Mango & Coconut Cream on Rye Toast with Roasted Cashews

Serves 2

kcal — 526
carbs — 36.0g
protein — 6.0g
fat — 39.8g

10 min

The coconut cream and tropical flavours in this dish are perfect for the summer months. The rye bread soaks up the juices perfectly.

400ml (14fl oz) can coconut milk (chilled in the refrigerator overnight)

½ tsp cinnamon

1 tsp vanilla extract

1 tbsp golden syrup + 1 tsp to drizzle

zest and juice of ½ lime (reserve half of the zest and juice for drizzling and garnishing)

2 slices of seeded rye bread

1 large ripe mango, peeled, stoned and finely sliced into half-moon slices

small handful of roasted cashews, crushed

Open the can of chilled coconut milk. The cream and milk will have separated overnight. Scoop out the cream and place it in a food processor (reserve the milk for making curry, or another recipe).

Add the cinnamon, vanilla extract, golden syrup and lime zest and juice to the food processor. Blitz to combine and whip the coconut cream to form soft peaks. Set aside.

Toast the rye bread to your liking, then spread the coconut cream over the toast. Layer the mango slices on top of the cream to make a lattice pattern.

Sprinkle over the crushed cashews and reserved lime zest and juice and serve.

Coconut Milk Puddings with Nut & Sesame Seed Topping

Makes 9

kcal — 238
carbs — 22.7g
protein — 3.0g
fat — 15.5g

10 min + 1 hour

2 min

These little puddings are like plant-based, wobbly panna cotta. They are a great make-ahead dessert, perfect for entertaining.

1 litre (1¾ pints) coconut milk drink

coconut cream from a 400g (14oz) can coconut milk (see left)

3 tsp agar agar powder

3 tbsp golden caster sugar

To serve

handful of roasted salted peanuts

handful of roasted cashews

3 tbsp toasted sesame seeds

2 tbsp toasted dried coconut flakes

2 tbsp golden caster sugar

condensed coconut milk

9 rose petals or other edible flowers

Place the coconut milk drink in a wok over a medium heat. Warm through, then add the coconut cream and stir to combine. Add the agar agar and stir to dissolve, then add the sugar and, again, stir to dissolve. Pass the mixture through a sieve and divide it between nine small circular ramekins (5cm/2in deep and 5cm/2in wide). Transfer to the refrigerator and chill for 1 hour to set. Meanwhile, grind the peanuts and cashews in a pestle and mortar. Stir in the toasted sesame seeds, coconut flakes and sugar. Set aside.

To serve, remove the puddings from the refrigerator. Place the ramekins in a tray of hot water to loosen, then tip each pudding on to a serving plate. Drizzle with condensed milk and sprinkle over the ground nut mixture. Top with a rose petal or edible flower.

Chocolate, Orange & Goji Berry Brownie Cakes

kcal — 374
carbs — 52.0g
protein — 7.1g
fat — 15.8g

Serves 12

15 min   45 min

Not only is this dessert easy to make, it's also high in antioxidants, thanks to the cacao and goji berries (which also add a delightful sweetness). The orange gives a zesty lift and makes this more-ishly delicious. I like to top it with lots of fresh raspberries for added vitamin C.

olive oil spread, for greasing

100g (3½oz) plain flour

50g (1¾oz) cacao powder

2 tsp baking powder

1 tsp ground cinnamon

½ tsp sea salt

4 tbsp chia seeds

8 tbsp cashew butter

125g (4½oz) light brown sugar

250ml (9fl oz) unsweetened almond milk or nut milk of your choice

2 tsp vanilla extract

zest of 2 oranges

100g (3½oz) dark chocolate chips

50g (1¾oz) dried goji berries

For the icing

40g (1½oz) cacao powder

250g (9oz) icing sugar

50g (1¾oz) vegetable shortening

125ml (4fl oz) unsweetened almond milk

200g (7oz) fresh raspberries, to garnish

Preheat the oven to 180°C/160°C fan/350°F/Gas Mark 4. Grease and line a 20cm (8in) square, 6cm (2½in) deep baking tin with baking paper.

Sift the flour, cacao powder, baking powder and ground cinnamon into a large mixing bowl. Add the salt and mix well to combine, making sure there are no lumps.

In a small jug or cup, mix the chia seeds with 8 tbsp water and let stand for 5 minutes. This will make a chia 'egg'.

In a food processor or using a hand-held mixer, cream together the cashew butter and sugar until smooth. Add the almond milk and mix well. Add the chia 'egg' and vanilla extract. Mix well again.

Tip the wet ingredients into the bowl of dry ingredients and mix well to create a smooth batter. Once smooth, add the orange zest, dark chocolate chips and goji berries and mix well.

Pour the batter into the prepared baking dish and bake in the centre of the oven for 45 minutes.

Remove from the oven and let cool on a wire rack for 30 minutes before decorating.

To make the icing, sift the cacao powder and sugar into a mixing bowl. Transfer to a food processor and add the vegetable shortening. Blitz to combine, then gradually add the almond milk, mixing well between additions, to create a smooth icing.

Transfer the cooled brownie cake to a serving dish and spread the icing over the top. Scatter over the fresh raspberries and serve.

Apple & Cinnamon Cake

kcal — 207
carbs — 31.0g
protein — 2.1g
fat — 9.1g

Serves 10

12 min   45 min

This cake is a simple favourite of ours at home. Use fresh, organic apples, or substitute with plums, damsons, pears, cherries or bananas. This recipe is so versatile, super easy and not too sweet, either. You will definitely want seconds!

olive oil spread, for greasing

200g (7oz) plain flour

1 tsp baking powder

1½ tsp ground cinnamon

½ tsp ground nutmeg

75ml (2½fl oz) rapeseed oil

100g (3½oz) golden caster sugar

150ml (5fl oz) nut milk of your choice

2 tsp vanilla extract

1 tbsp apple cider vinegar

2 gala apples, cored, each one sliced into 6 wedges

icing sugar (optional)

Preheat the oven to 180°C/160°C fan/350°F/Gas Mark 4. Line the base of a 22cm (8½in) round cake tin with baking paper and grease the sides.

Sift the flour, baking powder, cinnamon and nutmeg into a mixing bowl and stir to combine.

In a jug, mix together the rapeseed oil and golden caster sugar. Add the nut milk of your choice, along with the vanilla extract and apple cider vinegar. Stir to mix well.

Pour the wet ingredients into the dry ingredients and stir well to make a smooth batter.

Pour the batter into the prepared cake tin. Arrange the apple slices on top of the batter in a circular pattern.

Bake in the centre of the oven for 45 minutes. You will know it's ready when a skewer inserted into the centre comes out clean. Remove from the oven and leave to cool completely in the tin.

Once cool, transfer to a serving plate, dust with icing sugar (if using) and serve.

Mango & Cashew 'Cheese' Cake

kcal — 346
carbs — 30.9g
protein — 7.9g
fat — 21.1g

Serves 10

15 min
+
30 min
chilling

3 min

This is my fresh, light and fruity plant-based 'cheese' cake. The 'cheese' layer is made by blending cashew nuts with coconut cream and coconut yogurt. It is so simple, easy and straightforward, and definitely a family-friendly crowd pleaser. Don't let the timings put you off: there is plenty of time to relax while it's chilling.

For the biscuit base

200g (7oz) fruity vegan oat biscuits

3 tbsp mixed nut butter

For the cashew 'cheese' layer

200g (7oz) cashews, soaked in water for 30 minutes, then drained and rinsed

200ml (7fl oz) coconut milk (see tip on page 67)

400g (14oz) plain coconut yogurt

1 tbsp coconut cream

3 tbsp golden syrup

juice of 1 lime

pinch of sea salt

For the fresh mango compote

2 mangos, peeled, stoned and diced into 0.5cm (¼in) cubes

4 tbsp golden syrup

To garnish

zest and juice of 1 lime

To make the biscuit base, crush the biscuits in a food processor. Add the nut butter and process until well combined. Transfer the mixture to a bowl and set aside. Clean the food processor.

Place all the cashew 'cheese' layer ingredients in the food processor and blend until smooth.

Line the base of a 26cm (10½in) round glass cheesecake dish with the biscuit and nut butter mixture and press into place. Pour over the blended cashew 'cheese' mixture. Cover and let it set in the refrigerator for 30 minutes.

Meanwhile, make the mango compote. Place the mango and golden syrup in a shallow frying pan over a medium heat. Stir gently to combine. Cook for 2–3 minutes until the mango has softened and the mixture is slightly sticky. Take off the heat and let cool for 30 minutes.

To assemble, remove the 'cheese' cake from the refrigerator and top with the cooled mango compote. Just before serving, garnish with the lime zest and juice. Enjoy!

Open Ice Cream Sandwich

5 min

Serves 4

kcal — 251
carbs — 34.5g
protein — 6.1g
fat — 10.1g

The condensed coconut milk in this dish is an absolute dream. You can buy the sweet red adzuki bean paste from Japanese or Asian supermarkets, but this dessert still works without if you can't get it.

2 slices of thick white bread

2 tbsp crunchy peanut butter

2 tbsp sweet red adzuki bean paste (optional)

4 scoops vegan chocolate ice cream

2 tbsp condensed coconut milk, chilled (stir together if it has separated in the can)

sour cherries, to garnish (optional)

Toast your favourite chunky white bread until golden. Slice each piece of bread in half to give 4 triangles in total.

Slather on some peanut butter, followed by some the sweet red adzuki bean paste. Top each piece of bread with a scoop of vegan chocolate ice cream, drizzle over the cold condensed coconut milk and garnish with some sour cherries, if using.

Chocolate Date Oat Bites

10 min
+
30 min
chilling

Makes 16 bites

kcal — 142
carbs — 23.0g
protein — 2.6g
fat — 5.0g

These oat bites make a perfect snack – they are like sweet, raw, oat-y, date-y flapjacks. They are simple to make, and you can keep them chilled or at room temperature, ready for whenever you have a sweet craving.

230g (8¼oz) oats

200g (7oz) pitted dates

3 tbsp cacao powder

3 tbsp golden syrup

¼ tsp sea salt

4 tbsp coconut cream

100ml (3½fl oz) coconut milk (see tip on page 67)

50g (1¾oz) dark chocolate, grated into shavings

Line a 20cm (8in) square, 6cm (2½in) deep baking tin with baking paper. Place 200g (7oz) of the oats in a food processor along with the dates, cacao powder, golden syrup, sea salt, coconut cream and coconut milk. Blitz well to combine.

Transfer the mixture the prepared baking tin and chill in the refrigerator for 30 minutes.

Remove from the refrigerator and dust over the remaining 30g (1oz) oats and the chocolate shavings. Slice into 5cm (2in) squares. Serve immediately or store in an airtight container in the refrigerator or at room temperature. They will keep for 2 weeks if stored in the refrigerator, or 1 week at room temperature.

Raspberry & Chocolate Avocado Pudding Pots

kcal — 238
carbs — 15.2g
protein — 2.8g
fat — 18.9g

Serves 4

10 min
+
30 min
chilling

These chocolate avocado pudding pots are to die for: good for you and tasty. The smooth, velvety quality of the mixture also makes it perfect as a ganache-like topping on a chocolate cake. Feel free to vary the toppings with your favourite fruits or chopped nuts.

2 ripe avocados, peeled and stoned

3 tbsp cacao powder

3 tbsp golden syrup

1 tbsp date syrup

3 tbsp coconut milk (see tip on page 67)

1 tsp vanilla extract

¼ tsp sea salt

1 tbsp raw cacao nibs, plus extra to serve

1 tbsp toasted coconut flakes

4 fresh raspberries

Place the avocado flesh in a food processor, along with the cacao powder, golden syrup, date syrup, coconut milk, vanilla extract and sea salt. Process until smooth, then stir in the cacao nibs.

Divide the mixture between four ramekins or individual dishes with a depth and width of 4cm (1½in). Transfer to the refrigerator and chill for 30 minutes until firm.

To serve, sprinkle over some more cacao nibs and the toasted coconut flakes. Top each pudding with a raspberry and eat immediately.

Asian Pantry

From sriracha and oyster to garlic hoisin, you can create sweet, sour, spicy sauces and dressings that will complement your dishes, whether you use them as cook-in sauces or dressings on the side. Think of your condiment cupboard like a bar, where you are the mixologist, creating your own sauces and producing a cocktail of stir-fry flavours – so go crazy!

Know your oils

For stir-frying, use a heat-stable oil such as coconut, rapeseed or peanut oil. For salad dressings, opt for extra virgin olive oil. Toasted sesame oil is for dips, dressings and seasoning, usually at the end of cooking.

Soybean sauces

I can't live without my soybean pastes, from fermented salted yellow bean (or whole beansin a jar), chilli bean, fermented salted dried black bean (soybeans dried and salted in the sun – just give them a rinse in water, then crush and mix into Shaohsing rice wine to make a paste), to Japanese salty miso paste (which comes in red and white varieties – great for soups, stir-fries, sauces, dressings and marinades), and the Korean chilli paste gochujang, which, together with the Korean yellow bean paste, doenjang, is one of my favourites. The flavour combinations are limitless, with endless umami (deep savoury) possibilities.

Curry pastes

I love to experiment with Southeast Asian curry pastes such as Thai red curry, Thai green curry, yellow curry and so on, and not just to make curry, but for stir-frying and in noodle soups. I also love chilli pastes and sambals from Malaysia, as well as spice mixes and tamarind paste, which give a sour kick and an exotic Southeast Asian taste to my dishes. Making your own is simple too, just blitz the aromatics in a food processor. Some pastes come vegan friendly, too, without the fish sauce, so always check the label.

Spice it up

Use your spices and get creative. My two go-tos are: Chinese five spice (a combo of Sichuan peppercorns, star anise, fennel, cinnamon and cloves) and Xian-inspired (a blend of dried chillies, fennel, cumin and sea salt – the perfect rub on meaty mushrooms or on corn). To get the best out of your spices, particularly whole spices, first dry toast them in a wok or pan and then grind in a pestle and mortar or coffee grinder.

Rice and grains, baby!

Jasmine rice is my rice of choice, but you can use any you like. Sometimes, when I'm trying to eat more healthily, I mix jasmine rice, wild rice and green lentils. At other times, I serve it plain, for comfort. Basmati is a good option for fried rice, as it is more robust. Brown rice is also delicious and high in fibre. It can be mixed with jasmine rice, wild rice and chickpeas to create a different bite. So, it's up to you how you rice!

Use your noodle

It's best to pre-cook noodles according to the packet instructions, then drain and drizzle some toasted sesame oil over to prevent them from sticking together. For low-carb and wheat-free options, try mung bean noodles, sweet potato noodles or shirataki and rice noodles. I also love the traditional wheat-flour noodles, which come in several varieties, such as buckwheat, somen, ramen and udon. For a high-protein variety, try using soybean noodles. I have a range with Yutaka that is organic and gluten-free.

Go sweet and sour

Make your own sauce combinations by using fresh juices from apples, oranges, pineapple, mango, grapes, lemons or limes and combine them with soy sauce/tamari, chilli flakes and golden syrup (a vegan alternative to honey) to create flavourful dishes. I like to use apple cider vinegar, black and clear rice vinegar, which is a must-have in my pantry too. To add sweetness, I use golden granulated sugar, maple syrup, golden syrup, date syrup and agave syrup.

Go nutty

Nuts are a healthy source of fats, high in protein and a good source of minerals, omega-6 and vitamin E, which promotes healthy skin. A small handful is enough. You can roast or toast your own for an added layer of flavour. My favourites are cashews, almonds and pine nuts, which I find best complement savoury stir-fries as they are sweeter. For salads, I like to use walnuts and Brazil nuts, as they are chunkier and have a satisfying texture against leafy salads. My favourite seeds are sesame, linseeds, pumpkin, sunflower and flaxseeds.

Cornflour/potato flour

Cornflour or potato flour helps to bind the flavours in the wok to the protein and vegetables.

Traditionally, when cooking meat, a technique called 'velveting', where egg white and cornflour are combined to make a batter when shallow-fried, was the norm. I've designed a new way to enhance flavour without shallow-frying. First, season the ingredient with salt and ground white pepper, then dust with cornflour or potato flour. This helps to seal in the juices. To make sure it doesn't stick to the wok, let it brown for a few seconds and then you can easily toss it. Don't worry if it catches – those slightly burnt edges add to the flavour. You can loosen the flavours by using a drop of water or Shaohsing rice wine.

In some of my dishes, cornflour is mixed with cold water to create a paste that is usually added at the end to thicken the sauce and give it a shine as it comes to the boil. In many dishes, where I group ingredients together for a more complex flavour, I add the cornflour to the sauce ingredients. Ensure that the main liquid in the sauce, whether it's water or vegetable stock, is cold, so that the sauce thickens in the wok rather than before in the jug.

A Cook's Notes

Aromatics

Garlic, ginger, chillies and spring onion are full of antibacterial, antifungal properties, and create incredible layers of flavour. I love to blitz them in a food processor, pour over some sesame oil and keep in a jar in the refrigerator so they're ready to add to stir-fries, curries, soups and salad dressings. You can of course mix it up with lemongrass, shallots, onions and coriander roots.

Magic mushrooms

Mushrooms are incredibly versatile, give a delicious meaty taste and are full of antioxidants. Use a variety, such as enoki, shimeji, king trumpet, shiitake and chestnut mushrooms, to create different textures. If you are feeling lazy, drizzle over some oil, add a pinch of salt and roast them for 8 minutes at 180°C (350°F) – it makes them perfect for adding to noodles, salads, soups or rice. Dried shiitake mushrooms are yum, too, and have an earthy, savoury umami flavour.

Eat your greens

I use everything from long-stem broccoli to Brussels sprouts, spinach and pak choi. All these vegetables are high in antioxidants, vitamins, minerals and fibre. They help prevent obesity, heart disease and high blood pressure. Use the freshest produce possible so they keep their colour and texture once cooked.

Salt the oil

Many Chinese chefs believe that seasoning the oil with a pinch of salt before adding the aromatics helps to retain the colour of the vegetables. I like this method as it means the salt flavour is evenly distributed throughout, and you avoid having large, undissolved flakes of salt in the finished dish.

Water is your best friend

Use filtered water for the recipes as it gives a cleaner taste. Always have a small jug of water to hand when stir-frying, so you can add a drop when the the ingredients are starting to burn. You will also need water if you are making a one-wok dish where you 'don't return' (in Mandarin, *hui guo*) the ingredients to the wok, as you will need to deglaze between additions to help each group of ingredients cook. Generally, this needs to be done after the protein has been cooked and again once the vegetables have gone in. When stir-frying tender leaf vegetables, after adding the oil and aromatics, a little water around the edge of the wok helps to steam the vegetables, ready for seasoning.

Gluten-free

Many dishes are gluten-free if you use tamari instead of low-sodium light soy sauce and you omit wheat gluten/wheat-flour noodles. There are gluten-free substitutes, so look out for specialist producers online.

Nutrition

The nutritional analysis of kcal, carbs, protein and fat is per portion.

Equipment

Apart from a good flat-bottomed wok (like my Lotus Wok) and wok lid, all you need is an all-purpose chef's knife (or Chinese cleaver), a chopping board and a wooden spatula for stir-frying. I also find a small food processor is great for making spice pastes, a blender for smoothies and juicer for juicing.

Wok Your Heart Out

For me, the healthiest way to sear food is at a high heat – stir-frying retains the nutrients and extracts maximum flavour with minimum effort. Steaming is also such an easy way to retain nutrients in veggies. I mostly call upon these two techniques for the recipes in this book. If I want more veg in a particular meal, I will often steam an assortment and have them alongside the dishes I'm cooking. Just go with the flow and be flexible. That is the best way to cook.

For those who want to master the wok, below are some tips about the different techniques and what you can do to get the full creative use out of this magical cooking pot.

Choosing a wok

Most professional Chinese chefs use unseasoned carbon steel woks but they need a lot of love and care or they rust. Non-stick varieties, however, are not ideal since the coating comes off with time. If you are really into healthy eating, a stainless-steel wok, which can be seasoned with apple cider vinegar, is best, though stainless steel sometimes has uneven heat spots and food can stick, plus it doesn't retain heat as well as carbon steel. Aluminium woks are inexpensive but they can rust and warp and are not as good conductors of heat as carbon steel woks. My grandmother used to cook on a cast-iron wok and they are the best, but they are heavy and it can be difficult to toss the food or manoeuvre them away from the hob when the heat gets too high.

Traditional woks are round-bottomed but these require a wok ring set over your stove, which is not ideal, particularly for induction hobs. Some carbon steel woks have a flat, wide base more like a saucepan, which is not a traditional wok shape, so look for ones with deep sides (to allow you to toss the food) and a small centre (to concentrate the heat).

Whatever wok you have, however, it's best to use it and not waste it.

When you need a replacement, please do seek out my Lotus wok, which is made from carbon steel so that it heats quickly, plus it has a natural, 'non-stick'-type, nano-silica coating (made from sand-blasted crystals). It is a medium gauge, so not too heavy yet not flimsy. It's also scratch resistant, so you can use metal utensils on it, and hydrophobic, which means it repels water, giving your veggies that crisp finish, and oleophilic, which means it allows just enough oil to coat the surface of the wok. It is a clever wok that just gets better with time – I have used mine for over three years now and it is still going strong. It comes with a wooden spatula, a glass lid and a stainless steel steamer rack. You can purchase it on Amazon.com or for more information check out www.chinghehuang.com

If you don't need to season your new wok, just use a damp sponge and a little soapy water to wash off any industrial oil, dust or dirt, then place on the heat to dry. If you need to season your wok, go to my online video at www.youtube.com/user/chinghehuang, which shows you how.

The 'breath of the wok'

This is the term used to describe the *wok-hei* – the 'smoky flavour' – that comes from a good flame-wokked dish and the all-important balance of *xiang, se, wei* (the aroma, colour and taste of the overall dish). This is where home wok cooking differs from restaurant wok cooking. Restaurant wok burners can reach heats of 650°C (1,200°F), far higher than the 180°C (350°F) that the average domestic hob can achieve, although some powerful domestic burners can go as high as 400°C (750°F).

Wok chefs in restaurants manoeuvre and operate a gas lever by the side of their legs at the same time as they toss the wok and flick it towards the flames so they lick the sides of the wok, injecting wok smoke into the dish. This is why I have so much respect for wok chefs – they have no fear of the flames, which can sometimes be over 2m (6½ft) high. They inject the breath of the wok into the dish, as well as sauté, sear, deep-fry, shallow-fry, steam, braise, all in one cooking vessel, and have the eye-to-hand-to-leg body co-ordination (the wok dance) to time the addition of each ingredient perfectly. Cooking on such high heat means that if you are 1 second out your vegetables lose their shine or crispness and is why perfect stir-frying is so hard to master. Consistent results take practice, timing, skill and unwavering focus. However, this doesn't mean that you can't still get those smoky, delicious results from wokking at home!

Stir-frying

This is the classic use for a wok – a little bit of oil and lots of stirring ensures that ingredients keep their crunch and take on a delicious smoky flavour. The following tips will help you get it as perfect as possible.

Preparation is king. When it's 'wok on', there is no time to do anything, least of all to stop and chop, so you need to ensure that all your ingredients are prepped beforehand and as close to the wok as possible. Your ingredients should also be as fresh as possible; if they're substandard you will be able to tell, because, once stir-fried, they will go limp very quickly.

The right oils

Use an odourless, flavourless oil that has a high heat point, such as rapeseed, peanut or coconut oil as it gives a neutral base on which to create layers of flavour, yet can withstand high temperatures.

How hot a wok?

Your wok needs to be really hot before you add anything – you should see a little smoke rising off the surface. At that point, it's time to quickly add the oil, which will heat up instantly. Heating the wok first means the heat is evenly distributed over the surface. Once you add ingredients to it, the temperature will fall, but you need to keep the ingredients moving to prevent them burning, or to take the wok away from the heat. If you are worried about the flame, heat the wok over a medium–high heat and work your way up to maximum heat over the course of several stir-fries until you become more proficient.

Be quick with the aromatics

Once the wok is hot, and the oil is in, quickly add your aromatics and follow speedily with the next ingredient to prevent it from burning. You have to wok fast and preparation is key! I have been accused of adding garlic, ginger and chillies in almost all my dishes, but this is because I try to inject their healthful, antibacterial properties into my cooking as much as possible.

Size and shape matter

When adding several ingredients to the wok at the same time – for example, aromatics or different types of vegetable – they need to be of a similar size to ensure they cook in the same amount of time.

Also consider the size of the main protein ingredient in relation to the rest of the ingredients. For example, if you are wokking tofu slices, make sure the vegetables are cut in slices too, so that the dish looks balanced. How you cut your ingredients is crucial, too. If you slice on a deep diagonal, it exposes more surface area for cooking and can make ingredients go further. A carrot, for example, can be sliced into round coins or long oval pieces.

'Compartment' cooking

A dish can sometimes look like it has a lot of ingredients but most are usually storecupboard ingredients and garnishes, so the list will not be as long as it first appears, particularly if you group your ingredients, for example aromatics, vegetables and seasonings. Think of your protein separately – what flavours are you trying to achieve? Finally, think of your garnishes and ways to inject some freshness.

Steaming

Food cooked in this way is super healthy! You can use a bamboo steamer set in a wok, or stainless steel or bamboo racks set on top of a wok and all you have to do is pop the lid on. Bamboo steamers are versatile, as you can pile a few compartments on top of each other to steam multiple dishes at once. While steaming they also give off a light bamboo fragrance. The stainless steel rack lasts a lot longer.

Before you start, make sure your wok is stable. If you have a flat-bottomed wok, wobble won't be a problem, but if you have a round-bottomed one, you will need a wok stand. And before you attempt to take off the lid of a steamer, take care to turn the hob off first and gently lift the lid away from you, so the hot steam doesn't burn your arms. Safety first!

How much water do I fill the wok with?

Fill the wok half-full of water and place the bamboo steamer on the top, making sure the base does not touch the water. Depending on the recipe, place the food on a heatproof plate or shallow bowl that fits inside the steamer, on greaseproof paper or on pieces of food (for example, dumplings can be set on top of small slices of carrot for presentation purposes). Put the lid on and steam. If necessary, top up with more boiling water as the food cooks. The trick is make sure the bamboo steamer or rack you are using is stable, fits comfortably and securely within the wok and there is minimal opportunity for steam to escape. The key is to find a steamer that is big enough to steam a large amount and also fits snugly across the wok. You can pile up to three bamboo steamers high; any more and you may need a more powerful burner to create enough steam.

Deep-frying

Deep-frying gets a bad rap as it's deemed an unhealthy way of cooking. It isn't as healthy as a steamed dish or even a stir-fry, but it is not as bad as you might think. If food is dropped in hot enough oil, the outside edges are sealed at high temperatures and so the latent heat continues to cook the food, and doesn't allow further oil to be absorbed into the food.

So the most important tip – apart from having a stable and secure wok – is to make sure the oil is at the correct temperature. For best results invest in a deep-frying thermometer and follow the recommended temperatures in my recipes. If the oil is not hot enough, the food will be greasy and will take longer to cook. If the temperature is too high, the food will burn on the outside and remain raw inside. If you don't have a thermometer, use the ginger or bread test – add either a cube of bread or small piece of ginger and, if it turns golden brown within 15 seconds, the oil is at 180°C (350°F).

Use a slotted spoon or a Chinese 'spider' – a web-like mesh scoop – to lift out fried food as it helps to drain much of the oil in the process, then place the food onto a plate lined with kitchen paper. Spiders come in various sizes and are available in Chinese supermarkets. Other important rules are:

- Make sure your wok is stable.
- Never fill your wok more than half-full of oil, to avoid the chance of it bubbling over.
- Ensure your ingredients aren't wet as they will spit in the hot oil.
- For fresher results, avoid reusing oil.
- Use large tongs or long wooden bamboo chopsticks to help turn the food. Don't use plastic utensils, as they will melt.

Lastly, serve the dish immediately, as it will start to lose its crunch and crispness. If unavoidable, keep the food hot in a preheated oven before serving.

Braising

I've included a few recipes that require a quick braise. You can either wok-fry the ingredients and then add some stock and the seasonings for a quick saucy or brothy dish. The deep sides of a wok allow you to add as much liquid as you want and then, at the end of cooking, there is room to add noodles. As with all wokking, make sure the wok is stable on the hob.

Boiling

With its deep sides, a wok is perfect for boiling. It works just like a large pot and is great for soups and broths, so you can boil away to your heart's content!

Smoking

Smoking is not a technique I use in this book but it can be useful to smoke a block of tofu. Set the wok on hot fruit wood chips, jasmine rice or whatever flavours you like. Place a stainless steel rack on top with the tofu in a heatproof plate on top of the rack. Close the lid, turn the heat to very low and let the ingredients at the base gently burn to create smoke.

Jasmine Rice

kcal — 308
carbs — 73.9g
protein — 5.6g
fat — 1.0g

Serves 4

5 min

15–20 min

My go-to favourite rice is jasmine: it has a sweet, nutty taste and aroma, and is perfect for soaking up delicious Asian flavours. This amount of rice serves four people, or you can halve the quantities to serve two. You can always keep any leftovers for fried rice the next day.

350g (12oz) jasmine rice

Place the rice in a heavy-based saucepan and add 600ml (20fl oz) water. Place over a high heat and bring to the boil, then cover with a tight-fitting lid, reduce the heat to low and cook for 15–20 minutes. Uncover the pan and remove from the heat. Fluff up the grains of rice with a fork and serve immediately.

Simple Seitan

kcal — 188
carbs — 13.7g
protein — 27.6g
fat — 2.7g

Serves 4, makes approx 250g (9oz)

10 min
+
20 min rest

1 hour

Seitan, which is made from wheat gluten, has been eaten across Asia for centuries by Buddhist monks and nuns. Highly nutritious, every 100g (3½oz) contains 22.5g (¾oz) protein, as well as minerals such as selenium and iron, so it is a good source of plant protein as long as you are not allergic to gluten. A great alternative to smoked and firm tofu, tempeh and mushrooms, it's a delicious accompaniment to veggies.

130g (4½oz) vital wheat gluten

2 tbsp wholewheat flour

1 tbsp vegetable bouillon powder

For the braising liquid

1 tbsp freshly grated root ginger

1 litre (1¾ pints) vegetable stock

1 tbsp miso paste

2 tbsp tamari or low-sodium light soy sauce

In a bowl, mix together the wheat gluten, flour and vegetable bouillon powder. Stir until combined. Add 250ml (9fl oz) water and mix to form a dough. Shape the dough into a round, but do not knead.

Cover with a clean tea towel and leave the dough to rest in the bowl for 20 minutes. Heat a wok or stockpot over a low heat. Add the ginger, vegetable stock, miso paste, tamari or light soy sauce and 1 litre (1¾ pints) water. Stir and bring to a gentle simmer. Carefully drop in the ball of dough.

Cover and simmer gently for 1 hour, allowing the seitan to absorb the flavour of the liquid. Remove from the heat and drain, reserving the liquid. Allow the seitan to cool.

You can slice the seitan to use it immediately, or refrigerate it in an airtight container, covered with the reserved braising liquid, for about 7–10 days. If you want to freeze the seitan, slice it and place it in an airtight container, then transfer to the freezer, where it will keep for about 6 months. You do not need to store it in the braising liquid if you are freezing.

Simple Tofu

Serves 4

8 min + overnight soaking

2 hours

Tofu – or *Doufu* in Mandarin Chinese – has been a staple in Chinese cuisine and all across Southeast Asia for centuries. It takes on the flavours and seasonings that it is cooked with, making it the most versatile ingredient in the Asian plant-based kitchen. It is low in sodium, low in calories, rich in protein, cholesterol-free, easily digestible and a source of all essential amino acids.

500g (1lb 2oz) dried soybeans

1 heaped tbsp nigari salt

Soak the soybeans in 1 litre (1¾ pints) water overnight.

The next day, drain the beans. Retain the soaking liquid – you can use it for soup or broths, or for cooking vegetables.

Rinse the beans well. Place half the beans in a blender with 750ml (25fl oz) water. Blend until the beans have turn into a pulpy liquid. Transfer to a jug. Repeat with the remaining beans and another 750ml (25fl oz) water.

In a small bowl or cup, mix the nigari salt with 2 tbsp of warm water and stir well to dissolve. Set aside.

Strain the pulpy raw soy 'milk'/blended water through a fine muslin cloth to separate out the fibre and pulp.

Pour the strained liquid into a large saucepan over a low–medium heat. Bring to the boil. This should take about 3–4 minutes, but watch it closely – this liquid can come to the boil very quickly, and you don't want to burn it. You may notice a 'skin' collecting on the surface. This is 'yuba' (see below). Skim this off and set aside.

Once the liquid has boiled, leave it to cool to about 80°C (176°F), then gently stir in the nigari salt mix, which will act as a solidifying agent. Leave to rest for 10–15 minutes.

Gently strain the mixture through a muslin cloth once again and transfer to a tofu mould lined with another muslin cloth. If you don't have a mould, place the tofu on a wire rack with a tray underneath. Place a square plate with a weight on top to press and drain the tofu. Leave the tofu to set and drain for 2 hours.

Once the tofu has set, cut it into square pieces and gently place them in a glass container filled with cold water. This will keep in the refrigerator for 7 days.

Soya milk and yuba (tofu 'skin') — This recipe also produces some delicious by-products. The yuba, or tofu 'skin' that forms when you are boiling the liquid, can be dehydrated in a low oven and used in soups and stir-fries. It's delicious and highly nutritious. And if you find you have more liquid than you need to fill your tofu mould, the rest is soy milk, and can be used in all the ways shop-bought soy milk is used.

Kimchi

kcal — 414
carbs — 66.8g
protein — 21.3g
fat — 7.4g

Makes 1.5 litres (2¾ pints, including the cabbage and juices)

Prep
15 min
+
6–8 hrs
soaking

Ferment
3 days–
2 weeks

Korean kimchi is a delicious side dish made from fermented, salted cabbage and radishes. It has a spicy, sour kick. The spice is from Korean red pepper flakes, known as gochugaru, and the tang comes from the fermentation. This is my all-time favourite pickle and it is so good for your gut bacteria. Traditional kimchi uses fish sauce, but my vegan version uses red miso paste to achieve that salty, umami taste. The mix gets better over time and is perfect in stews, stir-fries and noodle broths.

2 heads of Chinese cabbage

65g (2½oz) sea salt

1 daikon or mooli, peeled and sliced into julienne strips

3 spring onions, trimmed and cut into 5cm (2in) slices

2.5cm (1in) piece of fresh root ginger, peeled

8 garlic cloves, peeled

2 shallots, peeled

6 tbsp gochugaru (Korean red pepper flakes), or more if you like it spicier

2 tbsp red miso paste

2 tsp caster sugar

1 tbsp glutinous rice powder (optional)

Reserve 1–2 outer leaves of the cabbage. Wrap these leaves in dampened kitchen paper and place in the refrigerator until needed. Shred the remaining cabbage and place it in a large, deep pot or bowl. Add the salt and toss well. Add enough cool water to cover the cabbage and stir until the salt is dissolved. Place a plate over the bowl to keep the cabbage submerged and leave, at room temperature, for 6–8 hours or overnight (stir halfway through if possible).

Drain the cabbage, reserving the brine. Rinse the cabbage, squeeze out any excess water, then return it to the bowl, adding the daikon or mooli, radishes and spring onions. Place the ginger, garlic, shallots, Korean red pepper flakes, red miso paste and sugar in a food processor. Add the rice powder, if using, and pulse until the mixture forms a paste.

Scoop the paste over the cabbage and other vegetables. Using tongs or gloves, mix and massage the vegetables and paste together really well, until the vegetables are well coated.

Pack the mixture into a large, 2-litre (3½-pint) sterilised jar, leaving 2.5–5cm (1–2in) of space at the top to allow for the juices that will be created. Add enough of the reserved brine to just cover the vegetables, pressing them down a bit. Place the whole cabbage leaf or leaves over top, pressing down – this should help keep the kimchi submerged under the brine. You can also use a fermentation weight if you have one, placing it on top of the whole leaf to keep the kimchi submerged.

Cover loosely (to allow air to escape) and place the jar in a baking dish or large bowl, to collect any juices. The idea is to keep as much of the flavourful juice in the jar as possible, so resist the urge to overfill it!

Leave the jar on the kitchen work surface, out of direct sunlight, for 3 days. During this time, you can press down on the kimchi daily with the back of a wooden spoon to keep all the bits submerged.

After 3 days, the kimchi is ready, but it won't achieve its full flavour and complexity for about another 2 weeks, so I suggest you seal and transfer the jar to the refrigerator, where the kimchi will continue to slowly ferment. The longer you ferment it, the more complex the taste. The kimchi will keep in the refrigerator for months (as long as it is submerged in the brine). To serve, scoop out using a slotted spoon, transfer to a small side dish and dress with toasted sesame seeds. It is delicious on top of noodle soups, broths or stews, or added to a stir-fry before serving.

Ginger & Spring Onion
Infused Oil

kcal — 213
carbs — 2.7g
protein — 1.1g
fat — 22.0g

This is a very simple fresh seasoning ingredient that I like to keep in my fridge. If the Chinese came up with a 'salsa verde', I think this would be it. I like to pour the sesame oil over the top of the paste, to preserve the fresh paste and also to infuse the oil with the delicious flavours from the aromatics.

2.5cm (1in) piece of fresh root ginger, peeled

small bunch of spring onions, trimmed and roughly sliced into 2.5cm (1in) pieces

1 red chilli, with seeds

2 tbsp pure sesame oil

tamari or low-sodium light soy sauce, to serve

Place the ginger, spring onions and chilli in a small food processor. Blitz to create a roughly textured paste.

Transfer the paste into a small glass jar and push the paste down. Dress with the pure sesame oil.

To use, combine 1 tbsp of the paste with 1 tbsp tamari or light soy to make a fresh dipping sauce or stir fry sauce. Drizzle over your favourite stir-fries, curries, soups and salads.

Basic Recipes

Glossary

Adzuki red bean paste

Used as a dessert filling in Chinese cuisines, it is deep burgundy red in colour. To make it from scratch, the adzuki beans are cooked to a high temperature for 2 hours, puréed and sieved, then passed though a muslin cloth. The purée is then heated with sugar, and vegetable shortening is added to form a paste.

Apple cider vinegar

This is made by crushing apples and squeezing out the juice. The crushed material is submerged in a tank where oxygen is supplied and the first fermentation process is applied. Acetobacter and ethanol are added which give acetic acide and vinegar. The 'mother' is the microbial culture left in the vinegar before distilling and pasteurisation. Organic, unfiltered, naturally fermented apple cider vinegar that contains 'mother' contains strands of proteins, enzymes and friendly bacteria. Possible health benefits include improvements in arthritis and diabetes, reducing cholesterol and aiding weight loss.

Aquafaba

This is the viscous water retained from tinned chickpeas. It mimics the role of egg whites and is a great egg white replacement in plant-based dishes. Keep the water from tinned chickpeas in the refrigerator until ready to use.

Asparagus spears

These spring vegetables come in a variety of thicknesses and sizes. The shoots are prized for their sweet, nutty taste. They are a great source of fibre, folate and vitamins. They are delicious roasted, grilled or stir-fried.

Bamboo shoots

These add a crunchy texture to dishes. Boiled bamboo sprouts are also pickled in brine or chilli oil. Low in fat and sugar, they are a source of protein and fibre.

Beansprouts

These are crunchy and delicate, sprouted from mung beans, and a source of fibre, protein, vitamin C and folic acid.

Brown rice vinegar

This is made from unpolished brown rice and is reputedly richer in nutrients than polished rice vinegar. It is light brown in colour and is sweeter and less acidic than other vinegars. It can be found in health food stores or online.

Buckwheat/soba noodle

A Japanese noodle made from buckwheat ('soba' means 'buckwheat') and wheatflour, which gives it a dark brownish-grey color. They are medium in thickness and available in several varieties such as cha soba, made with tea leaves and buckwheat. You can find them in Asian markets, and they can be stored for 6–8 months. They make an ideal ingredient in a noodle salad. They are free from fat and cholesterol and a good source of manganese, protein, complex carbohydrates and thiamin. If 100 per cent buckwheat, they do not contain gluten.

Button mushrooms

These come in white or brown varieties and are also known as the common mushroom. They are an excellent source of B vitamins, riboflavin, niacin and pantothenic acid. They are also a good source of the mineral phosphorus.

Cashew butter

Made from baked or roasted cashews, this is a rich and creamy spread. It contains more carbohydrates and monounsaturated fat compared to peanut butter.

Chia seeds

Tiny black seeds from the *Salvia hispanica* plant, related to the mint family, which is native to Central and Southern Mexico. Once soaked, the seeds expand to 12 times their weight and develop a thick coating. Dry seeds contain 42 per cent carbohydrates, 16 per cent protein and 31 per cent fat. They are a rich source of B vitamins, thiamine, niacin, folate, and are also rich in calcium, iron, magnesium, phosphorus and zinc. The fatty acids are unsaturated with linolenic acid the majority fat. They can be mixed into smoothies, made into puddings and used as an egg replacement in baking.

Chilli bean paste

Made from broad beans and chillies that have been fermented with salt to give a deep brown-red sauce. Some versions include fermented soybeans or garlic. Good in soups and braised dishes; use this paste with caution, as some varieties are extremely hot.

Chilli oil

A fiery, orange-red oil made by heating dried red chillies in oil. To make your own, heat groundnut oil in a wok, add dried chilli flakes with seeds and cook for 2 minutes. Take off the heat and leave the chilli to infuse in the oil until completely cooled. Decant into a glass jar and store for a month before using. For a clear oil, pass through a sieve.

Chilli sauce/chilli garlic sauce

A bright red sauce made from chillies, vinegar, sugar and salt. Some varieties are flavoured with garlic and vinegar.

Chinese celery

This is more tender and has a more intense flavour than the Western variety. Both the stalks and leaves are used.

Chinese leaf/cabbage

This has a sweet aroma with a mild flavour that disappears when cooked. The white stalk has a crunchy texture and remains succulent even after prolonged cooking. It is used for kimchi.

Chinese chives (garlic chives)

These are long, flat, green leaves with a strong garlic flavour. There are two varieties; one has small yellow edible flowers at the top. Both are delicious. A good substitute is fine chives.

Chinese five spice powder

A blend of five spices – cinnamon, cloves, Sichuan peppercorns, fennel and star anise – that give the distinctive flavours of Chinese cooking.

Chinese wood ear mushrooms

A dark brown-black fungi with ear-shaped caps. Very crunchy in texture, they do not impart flavour but add colour and crispness. They should be soaked in hot water for 20 minutes before cooking – they will double in size.

Chinkiang black rice vinegar

A strong aromatic vinegar made from fermented rice. Mellow and earthy, it gives dishes a wonderful smoky flavour. Balsamic vinegar is a good substitute.

Chiu Chow chilli oil

Originating from the Chaozhou region of Southern China, this chilli oil has a unique taste and heat. Chewy and aromatic, it is made from a combination of preserved chillies in salt and garlic, soy, soybean and sesame oil.

Cinnamon stick/bark

The dried bark of various trees in the Cinnamomum genus. It can be used in pieces or ground. When ground it adds a sweet woody fragrance.

Congee

Plain soupy rice porridge that can be combined with other ingredients, such as salted peanuts, fermented bean curd and chilli-pickled bamboo shoots.

Coconut yogurt

Made from full fat coconut milk, the active probiotics in this yogurt supply key vitamins and minerals. The saturated fat, which is in the form of medium-chain triglycerides, can help control weight, reduce risk of atherosclerosis (plaque in the arteries) and boost immunity.

Condensed coconut milk – see Coconut milk

Coconut milk

Coconut milk is the diluted cream pressed out from the thick, white flesh of a well-matured coconut. Good coconut milk has a clean, white colour and tastes rich, creamy and mildly sweet. Natural coconut cream should rise to the top and separate from the heavier water component. Coconut cream is also available in tins and used in curries and desserts. Condensed sweet coconut milk is concentrated coconut milk and sugar used in desserts as syrup. Coconut milk contains high levels of iron, calcium, potassium, magnesium, and zinc, and good amounts of vitamins C and E, rich in lauric acid and monoglyceride fats.

Courgettes

Also known as 'the little squash', these vegetables are very versatile. Choose courgettes that are unblemished and firm. They do not need to be peeled and can be eaten raw. You can use them to make spiralised courgetti 'noodles', and they are delicious roasted, stir-fried, or in soups and curries. They are packed with nutrients from Vitamins C and A, potassium, folate and fibre.

Cumin

Cumin is the pale green seed of *Cuminum cyminum*, a small herb in the parsley family. Cumin has a distinctive, slightly bitter yet warm flavour. Ground cumin is stronger than whole seeds. It contains magnesium and iron.

Daikon (white radish)

Resembling a large white carrot, this crunchy vegetable has a peppery taste and pungent smell, and is eaten raw, pickled or cooked. It contains vitamin C and diastase, which aids digestion. Koreans use it to make kimchi.

Dofu/fresh bean curd

Described as the 'cheese' of China, this is made from soybean curd and takes on the flavour of whatever ingredients it is cooked with. Called tofu in Japan and dofu in Chinese, it is high in protein and also contains B vitamins, isoflavones and calcium. Available as firm, soft and silken, the firm variety is great in soups, salads and stir-fries. Silken has a cream cheese-like texture. Dofu gan is dried firm smoked beancurd.

Dark soy sauce – see Soy sauce

Dried Chinese mushrooms

These need to be soaked in hot water for 20 minutes before cooking. They have a strong aroma and a slightly salty taste and complement savoury dishes.

Dried folded flat rice noodles

These are naturally gluten-free and highly versatile. They are made from a paste of rice flour and water, then steamed, formed, cut and dried. To prepare boil a litre (1¾ pints) of water and soak the noodles in it for 5–10 minutes, drain and toss through some toasted sesame oil. These are used in the popular Thai stir fry – Pad Thai.

Dried wide knife-cut noodles

Made from wheatflour, these are also known as *Dao Xiao Mian* from the Shanxi province in China. Also known as knife shaved or knife cut noodles. You can buy the wide dried flat versions in Chinese supermarkets. Look for those made in Taiwan, China, which are the best quality.

Edamame beans

These are harvested while the beans are still attached to their branches (eda means 'branches' and mame 'beans' in Japanese). High in protein, they are cooked whole and the seeds are then squeezed out. They are rich in complete protein, fibre, vitamins and minerals.

Enoki mushrooms

Tiny, long-stemmed mushrooms with a delicate flavour. Used raw, they add texture to salads. Lightly steamed, they are slightly chewy. They are virtually fat free, provide complex carbohydrates and are high in B vitamins. They also contain pantothenic acid, riboflavin, folate, potassium and phosphorus.

Fennel seeds

Fennel is a strong aromatic spice that has a slight aniseed flavour. Delicious when toasted or pan-fried.

Fermented salted black beans

Small black soybeans preserved in salt. Rinse in cold water before use. They are used to make black bean sauce.

Fermented yellow bean paste

Made from yellow soybeans, water and salt. A substitute would be hoisin sauce, though this is sweeter and not as salty.

Flaxseed

High in omega-3 fatty acids, full of both soluble and insoluble fibre.

Galangal

This is a rhizome with culinary and medicinal uses and is best known in the West today for its use in Thai cuisine. It resembles ginger in appearance and taste with an extra citrus aroma. It is available as a powder or whole and can be found in most Asian supermarkets.

Glutinous rice

A type of rice grown and widely eaten all across Southeast and East Asia. It does not contain gluten – the name is because of its sticky nature. It has opaque white grains.

Goji berry (Chinese wolfberry)

The deep red, dried fruit of an evergreen shrub. Similar to a raisin, it is sweet and can be eaten raw or cooked. Containing all essential amino acids, it has one of the highest concentrations of protein in all fruit. It also contains vitamin and carotenoids, has 21 trace minerals and is high in fibre.

Golden needles

Also known as dried lily bulbs, these are the unopened flowers of the daylily which has been used as a food and medicinal plant for over 2,000 years. They are available in Chinese supermarkets in a dried form and have a delicate musky-sweet flavour. Used in soup broths or garnish in stir-fries.

Hijiki seaweed

This contains the highest amount of calcium of any sea vegetable. Full of fibre and protein, as well as iodine, niacin, phosphorus, phytohormones, potassium and vitamins A, B and C.

Hoisin sauce

Made from fermented soybeans, sugar, vinegar, star anise, sesame oil and red rice, this is great used as a marinade and as a dipping sauce.

Inari pockets

Seasoned fried tofu pouches that can be filled with veggies, rice, avocado or on their own. They can be bought from specialist Asian supermarkets.

Jasmine rice

A long-grain white, silky rice originating from Thailand that has a nutty jasmine-scented aroma. Rinse before cooking until the water runs clear.

Jack fruit

A Southeast Asian fruit that has a mango/pineapple/banana taste. Can be found in tins in most supermarkets. Delicious in stir-fries and curries.

Kaffir lime leaves

The leaves of the citrus fruit native to tropical Asia. The leaves emit an intense citrus aroma.

King trumpet mushrooms

Dense and spongy when raw but have a savoury umami flavour once cooked and give a soft crunchy texture. The stalks can be shredded and stir-fried, and have a mild abalone-like flavour.

Kimchi

A Korean staple made from salted and fermented Chinese cabbage mixed with Korean radish, Korean dried chilli flakes, spring onions, ginger and *geotgal* (salted seafood). In my vegan version, I used red miso paste instead of seafood.

Kohlrabi

A German turnip, same species as broccoli, kale, cauliflower, Brussel sprouts, cabbage and gai lan (Chinese broccoli). It can be eaten raw or cooked. When raw it is crunchy and mildly spicy. Delicious in salads, pickled or stir-fried.

Korean chilli flakes (gochugaru)

Made by drying the chillies in the sun then crushing them, these vibrant red flakes impart a spicy taste with a hint of sweetness. A good substitute is dried chilli flakes.

Korean yellow bean paste (doenjang)

Similar to Chinese yellow bean paste and Japanese Miso, this is made from fermented soy beans and brine. It is also flavoured with garlic and sesame oil and mixed with Korean chilli paste to produce samjang sauce. Miso is available in supermarkets so use miso if you cannot find Korean doenjang.

Korean chilli paste (gochujang)

A savoury, sweet, fermented paste made from Korean red chilli powder, glutinous rice, and salt-and-barley malt powder. Soybeans are also sometimes used.

Lemongrass (citronella root)

A tough, lemon-scented stalk popular in Thai and Vietnamese cuisines. Look for lemon-green stalks that are tightly formed, firm and heavy with no bruising, tapering to a deeper green.

Lotus root

The stem of the lotus plant. Mild and sweet in flavour, delicious in soups, salads, stir-fries and curries. Once cooked, it has a tender bite like cooked potatoes. Wash them well, and a quick blanch is recommended before cooking.

Mock duck – see Seitan

Minced soy

Minced soy is made from soy flour and contains soy proteins. It is a healthy economic meat substitute and includes complete proteins which means it contains all the essential amino acids. Minced soy can be dried or ground in flakes. To prepare it, pour over hot boiled water and leave to rehydrate. Use in stir-fries and curries.

Mirin

A sweet Japanese rice wine similar to sake, with a lower alcohol content but a more sugar (which occurs naturally as a result of the fermentation process).

Miso paste

A thick Japanese paste made from fermented rice, barley, soybeans, salt and a fungus called *kojikin*. Sweet, earthy, fruity and salty, it comes in many varieties depending on the types of grains used. Organic red and yellow varieties are available in most supermarkets. A complete protein, containing all the essential amino acids; a probiotic food; rich in B-complex vitamins; contains calcium, iron, zinc, copper and magnesium.

Mung bean noodles

Made from the starch of green mung beans and water, these come in various thicknesses, vermicelli being the thinnest. Soak in hot water for 5–6 minutes before cooking. If using in soups or deep-frying, no pre-soaking is necessary. They become translucent when cooked.

Mushroom oyster sauce – see Oyster sauce

Nigari salt

These are magnesium chloride salt crystals, and are used to make tofu. It is the Japanese name for the bitter salt that is extracted from sea salt. It is also labelled as Japanese nigari. These can be bought from online stockists.

Nori (dried seaweed)

Sold in thin sheets, this is usually roasted until it turns black or purple-green. Used as a garnish or to wrap sushi. Once opened, a pack must be stored in an airtight container or it loses its crispness. If this happens, roast the sheets over an open flame for a few seconds until crisp. A good source of calcium, iron, zinc, vitamins B12 and C and iodine.

Oyster mushrooms

Soft and chewy with a slight oyster taste, this white, yellow or grey oyster-shaped fungi is moist and fragrant.

Pad thai noodles

Flat noodles, 5mm (¼in) wide, made from rice. They need to be soaked in hot water for 5 minutes before cooking.

Pak choi

A vegetable with broad green leaves, which taper to white stalks. Crisp and crunchy, it can be boiled, steamed or stir-fried. Contains vitamin A, C and K.

Panko breadcrumbs

Made from bread without crusts, these Japanese breadcrumbs have a crisp texture. Almost all are vegan, but some have honey added. If in doubt use dried breadcrumbs.

Perilla leaf

This leaf is a herb and perilla is a term for a different number of species in the mint family. Japanese cooking uses the shiso variety which is smaller and mintier in flavour than the rounded perilla leaves which are used by the Koreans. They have a fresh, liquorice/aniseedy flavour. In Chinese cuisine, it is a superfood, also used to treat a variety of ailments from food poisoning to depression. Usually eaten raw to wrap salad or rice. These can be found in Asian supermarkets. Wrap in dampened kitchen paper to keep them fresh and store in the vegetable compartment in the refrigerator.

Pickled sushi ginger

Also known as 'gari', this is a type of tsukemono 'Japanese' pickled vegetables. Made from thin sliced ginger, marinated in a solution of sugar and vinegar. Delicious on sushi rice.

Potato flour

A smooth, gluten-free flour made from potatoes that are steamed, dried and ground. It gives crispness when used to coat ingredients before frying.

Ramen

Noodles, invented in China, that are used in Japanese noodle soups. They come in various thicknesses and shapes, but most are made from wheatflour, salt, water and kansui (alkaline mineral water); the latter gives the noodles a yellow hue and a firmer texture.

Red miso paste – see Miso paste

Rice vinegar

A clear, mild vinegar made from fermented rice. Cider vinegar can be used as a substitute. Chinese black rice vinegar is a rich vinegar used in braised dishes and sauces, and with noodles. When cooked, it gives a smoky flavour with a mellow and earthy taste. Balsamic vinegar makes a good substitute.

Rock sugar (dried)

These large sugar crystals are slightly golden-yellow in colour. They are used like granulated sugar in Chinese cooking. Use half the quantity of soft brown sugar as a substitute.

Glossary

Sake

A fermented Japanese drink made from polished rice that is brewed in a similar way to wine. Its alcohol content ranges from 15–20 per cent.

Seaweed

Excellent source of iodine; rich in protein, calcium, vitamins A and B12 and omega-3 fatty acids.

Sesame seeds

These oil-rich seeds add a nutty taste and a delicate texture to dishes. Available in black, white/yellow and red varieties, toasted and untoasted.

Seasoned sushi rice vinegar

Also known as sushi vinegar. Made from rice vinegar with added salt, sugar and sake (sometimes mirin), it is ready to use to season just-cooked sushi rice. This can be bought in most supermarkets or online Asian stores.

Seitan

A vegetarian ingredient made from wheat gluten, soy, sugar, salt and oil. A good substitute is bean curd or tofu skin. The gluten or soy is created in sheets and then then rolled into coils. Sometimes the surface is stamped to give a goosebump appearance. Tins of mock duck and other mock meats can be found in most Asian supermarkets in oil. Great in soups and stir-fries.

Shaohsing rice wine

Made from rice, millet and yeast that has been aged for 3–5 years, it gives a bittersweet finish. Dry sherry makes a good substitute.

Shawarma-spiced seitan

You can make your own sharwarma spice (page 160) and coat it in home-made seitan (page 194), or buy this product ready to cook in supermarkets. Sharwarma contains spices such as cumin, coriander, paprika, cloves and allspice and is warming and delicious.

Shiitake mushrooms

These dark brown umbrella-shaped fungi are prized for their culinary and medicinal properties. The dried variety needs to be soaked in water for 20 minutes before cooking.

Shimeji (beech) mushrooms

These come in white or brown varieties, and have long stems and concave caps.

Sichuan peppercorns

Known as *Hua jiao* in Mandarin or 'flower pepper', these have a pungent, citrusy aroma. They can be wok-roasted, cooked in oil to flavour the oil, or mixed with salt as a condiment.

Soy sauce

Made from wheat and fermented soybeans, soy sauce is available in dark and light varieties. Dark soy sauce is aged for longer, and is mellower and less salty. Light soy sauce is used in China instead of salt. Wheat-free varieties, called tamari, are available, though salty. You can also buy low-sodium varieties.

Soybean noodles

Thin, gluten-free dried noodles that are rich in protein and low in fat. They yield about double the amount of wheat-flour noodles once rehydrated.

Spirulina

A type of blue-green microalgae, found in salt water, a cousin to seaweed and kelp. It is a nutrient-dense food packed full of vitamins includes vitamins A, C, E, B as well as calcium, magnesium, zinc and selenium. Vitamin C and selenium help protect cells from damage.

Sriracha chilli sauce

A hot sauce made from chilli peppers, distilled vinegar, garlic, salt and sugar. It is named after the coastal town of Si Racha, Eastern Thailand.

Smoked tofu – see Tofu

Ssamjang – see Korean yellow bean paste

Star anise

The fruit of a small evergreen plant, these are called *bajio* or 'eight horns' in Chinese. They have a distinct aniseed flavour and are one of the ingredients found in Chinese five spice powder.

Sushi rice

Usually called japonica – this is a white short-grain Japanese rice. Rinse in a sieve until the water runs clear to get rid of any starchy powder.

Sweet chilli sauce

You can make your own sweet chilli sauce by boiling fresh red chillies, adding sugar and cook down, then blitz in a food processor. Store in a jar for 1 week. Shop-bought is widely available.

Sweet potato thread noodles

Made from sweet potato starch and water, these are also known as sweet potato 'glass' noodles because of their transparency. Cook according to packet instructions as some vary in thickness. They are used in the Korean dish japcae, have a lovely slippery, slightly chewy texture, and contain zero fat.

Tahini

Made from soaking sesame seeds in water and then crushing them to separate the bran from the kernels. The crushed seeds are soaked in salt water, causing the bran to sink. The floating kernels are skimmed off the surface and toasted and ground to make an oily rich paste. Used in Middle Eastern cuisines and in hummus.

Tamari – see Soy sauce

Tamarind sauce/paste

The tamarind tree produces a pod-like fruit. The edible pulp is tart and used across Southeast Asia in curries.

Tempeh

A nutrient-dense soy product with a nutty mushroom flavour and chunky texture. It is fermented and is high in protein, vitamins and minerals. It contains prebiotics which can help improve digestive health and reduce inflammation. It supports oxidative stress, decreases cholesterol and improves bone health. It doesn't contain salt and is delicious marinated with soy – perfect grilled, wok-fried or in curries.

Thai green curry paste

A spicy curry paste from Thailand that uses fresh green chillies blended with shallots, coriander roots, galangal, lemongrass, salt, kaffir lime leaves, Thai basil, ground white pepper. Delicious for marinading, in stir-fries or curries. If you're vegan, check the ingredients.

Thai red curry paste

A spicy curry paste that uses fresh red chillies blended with garlic, shallots, coriander roots, galangal, lemongrass, salt, kaffir lime leaves, Thai basil, ground black pepper. Delicious for marinading, or in stir-fries and curries. If you're vegan, check the ingredients.

Thai basil

Widely used throughout Southeast Asia. Thai Basil leaves are also known as sweet basil, and have small, narrow purple stems and green leaves. They have an aniseedy-liquorice flavour and are a delicious garnish to finish Thai curries and stir-fries. Can be bought from supermarkets or Asian supermarkets. If you can't find them, leave them out.

Toasted sesame oil

Made from white pressed and toasted sesame seeds, this oil is used as a seasoning and is not suitable for use as a cooking oil since it burns easily. The flavour is intense, so use sparingly.

Tofu

This is made by boiling soy milk, adding a solidifying agent such as calcium sulfate, separating out the curds, and pressing the 'cheese' solids into moulds. Sometimes called 'soy cheese', the result is a smooth, textured ingredient.

Togarashi shichimi/Shichimi pepper flakes/Japanese pepper flakes (nana-iro togarashi)

A Japanese spice salt that contains ground red chilli pepper, ground Sichuan peppercorns, roasted orange peel, white and black sesame seeds, hemp seeds, nori and ground ginger.

Turmeric

A perennial plant belonging to the ginger family, native to India and the East Indies. The powder form comes from the underground stems and is used in curries to give a yellow colour. One of the strongest anti-inflammatories and anti-oxidants, according to Chinese medicine.

Vegan mayonnaise

To make vegan mayonnaise, blend silken tofu, olive oil, lemon juice, vinegar, Dijon mustard and salt in a food processor. Store-bought varieties are also available.

Vegetarian mushroom sauce

Sometimes known as mushroom oyster sauce – a salty seasoning sauce made from cooked-down mushrooms (it does not contain oysters and is a vegetarian version of oyster sauce). Choose one that is thick and has a glossy shine.

Vegetable shortening

Usually made from palm oil. As a more healthier alternative use half olive butter and half coconut oil as a substitute.

Vegetable bouillon stock powder

A natural flavour enhancer made from dehydrated vegetable stock. Delicious in soups, stews, sauces, curries.

Vermicelli mung bean noodles – see Mung bean noodles

Vermicelli rice noodle

Similar to vermicelli mung bean noodles, they come in many different widths and varieties. Before cooking, soak in hot water for 5 minutes. For salads, soak for 20 minutes. Add them dry for soups.

Vietnamese mint

With its peppery and hot minty taste, this can be used as a garnish. It is available in most Asian supermarkets. You can use fresh mint as a substitute.

Vietnamese soy sauce

Vietnamese soy sauce is also called Tuong. There are many different varieties and some that use soybean paste. Hac xi dau in Vietnamese likens to Chinese dark soy sauce and adds a salty taste and mahogany brown colour to dishes. Substitute with Chinese dark soy sauce.

Vietnamese rice paper

Also known as banh trang, made from white rice flour, tapioca flour and salt. The tapioca flour gives the rice paper its sticky and smooth texture. Comes dried in thin, crisp, translucent sheets. Plunge each one in warm water for 10 seconds to make it pliable to make rice paper 'summer' rolls. They can be filled with different fillings and eaten raw. Cover the rolls with slightly damp kitchen paper to prevent them drying out.

Wakame seaweed

Usually comes dried and needs to be soaked in warm water for 5 minutes. Dark green in colour, it tastes of the sea and is slightly mineral in flavour. Health benefits include lowering cholesterol, decreasing blood pressure, reducing blood sugar and aiding weightloss. Add to soups and salads or braised dishes.

Water chestnuts

The roots of an aquatic plant that grows in freshwater ponds, marshes and lakes, and in slow-moving rivers and streams. Unpeeled, they resemble a chestnut and have a firm, crunchy texture.

Wasabi

The wasabi plant is a Japanese horseradish. Wasabi paste is spicy and contains mustards and green colouring.

Wheat-flour noodles

Thin, white dried noodles. Don't confuse these with thick Japanese udon noodles.

Wheat-flour pancakes (fresh)

Made from wheatflour, water and salt and rolled in very thin discs, these are steamed before serving. They can also be found in the frozen or chilled sections of Asian supermarkets.

Wheatflour dumpling skins/wrappers

Made from salt, flour and water. These are used to make a dough that encases vegetable and meat fillings to make dumplings. Available ready made from Chinese supermarkets, frozen or fresh. When using, cover with a damp towel.

Whole dried red chillies

Hot and fragrant, these are usually sun-dried. You can grind the chillies in a pestle and mortar to give flakes.

Yellow bean sauce

Made from fermented yellow soybeans, dark brown sugar and rice wine, this is a popular ingredient in Sichuan and Hunan province in China. Yellow bean paste is thicker and is used in marinades and as a flavouring in savoury dishes.

UK/US Glossary

Ingredients

aubergine: eggplant
baby aubergines: baby eggplants
biscuits: cookies
broad beans: fava beans
caster sugar: superfine sugar
chickpeas: garbanzo beans
chicory: Belgian endive
Chinese leaf: nappa cabbage/
Chinese cabbage
cornflour: corn starch
coriander (fresh): cilantro
courgette: zucchini
dehydrated soy mince:
textured soy protein

French beans: string beans/
green beans
golden syrup: can substitute
corn syrup
groundnut oil: peanut oil
icing sugar: confectioners'
sugar/powdered sugar
long-stem broccoli: broccolini
mangetout: snow peas
Maris Piper: this is a UK
potato variety. Substitute
for a floury potato, such
as a russet
pak choi: bok choy

pea aubergines: Thai pea
eggplants
pepper (red/green/yellow):
bell pepper
plain flour: all-purpose flour
rapeseed oil: canola oil
rolled oats: old-fashioned oats
spring onion: scallion
stock: broth
wholemeal flour: whole-wheat
flour

Equipment

baking paper: parchment paper
baking tin: baking pan
cake tin: cake pan
griddle pan: grill pan
grill: broiler
kitchen paper: paper towels
kitchen foil: aluminum foil
muffin tin: muffin pan
muslin cloth: cheesecloth
roasting tray: roasting pan
sieve: fine mesh strainer
worksurface: countertop

Acknowledgements

I owe a big thank you to my publisher, Joanna Copestick, and my editorial director, Judith Hannam, for yet another beautiful book. I have wanted to write a plant-based book for some time, and thank you for sharing my vision. Your support means a great deal. Thank you to my literary agent, Heather Holden Brown, for waving your fairy godmother wand and making it happen. Thank you to the wider team at Kyle Books both in the UK and US. The talented team at Kyle – to my editor Jenny Dye and my copy editor Tara O'Sullivan for your attention to detail. Thank you to Evi O. Studio for the funky design.

To the incredibly talented Tamin Jones for the photography, and Aya Nishimura and Rosie Reynolds for the beautiful food styling, and of course the one and only Wei Tang for the props. Special thanks to Lucy Carter and Nic Jones for the production of the book.

This book is dedicated to all my fans who have followed me on my cooking journey from day one. I am grateful for your love and support, I am indebted. I hope that you will enjoy incorporating more veggies into your diet and that you find inspiration in this book for your personal food journey, whether you are a 'foodie' or wish to consume more compassionately. I would love to hear your plant-based experiences and stories, please do write to me at info@chinghehuang.com or @chinghehuang

Thank you to Michael Kagan at ICM Talent and all the powers at BBC, ITV, Food Network, NBC for continuing to give me opportunities and allowing me to share my cooking on telly.

To all my family and friends, near or far, you know who you all are. You are all my rock and my journey is as much yours through all the meals we have shared together.

For my mum and dad, it has not always been an easy life for our family. In your quest and courage to immigrate from Taipei to South Africa and then to the UK to create a better life for us, you have given us extraordinary experiences. I wouldn't change any of it. In a heartbeat, I would do it all again. Grateful for all of it – the yin and the yang.

This book is also for the sets of three grandparents – Wu, Huang and Longhurst – my angels, looking out for us, giving your love, strength and inspiration.

To Jamie, my husband, I am so lucky to have you in my life, and you are lucky to have a personal chef! You wok my world.